COINS OF GOLD

COINS OF GOLD

To Lori

Enjoy!

Barbara Raué
Barbara Raué

Copyright © 2010 by Barbara Raué.

Library of Congress Control Number: 2010908549
ISBN: Hardcover 978-1-4535-1990-5
Softcover 978-1-4535-1989-9
Ebook 978-1-4535-1991-2

All rights reserved. No part of this book may be reproduced or transmitted in any form or by any means, electronic or mechanical, including photocopying, recording, or by any information storage and retrieval system, without permission in writing from the copyright owner.

This book was printed in the United States of America.

To order additional copies of this book, contact:
Xlibris Corporation
1-888-795-4274
www.Xlibris.com
Orders@Xlibris.com

Contents

Chapter 1:	A Picture is Worth a Thousand Words	9
Chapter 2:	Four Leaf Clover	13
Chapter 3:	Bullets, Bullets Everywhere	25
Chapter 4:	School Days	32
Chapter 5:	There's a piece . . . there's Another One	37
Chapter 6:	The Great Depression	43
Chapter 7:	The Long Ride	47
Chapter 8:	Bridges, Bridges Everywhere	50
Chapter 9:	Seeing the Sites	65
Chapter 10:	Where Are You?	75
Chapter 11:	This is a Plane?	77
Chapter 12:	First Love	81
Chapter 13:	Water, Water Everywhere and Small Golden Coins No More	89
Chapter 14:	Oh the Anguish	96
Chapter 15:	My Eldest Son	99
Chapter 16:	Go Over, Go Under, Go Around, Or Go Through, But Never Give Up	109
Chapter 17:	Joy Everywhere	113
Chapter 18:	Second Chance at Love	119
Chapter 19:	Travel	131
Chapter 20:	Coins of Gold Flying From the Pouch	139
Chapter 21:	Celebrations	145
Chapter 22:	Goodbye, Mom	151

Golden Coins

A bag of golden coins is mine,
Each one is made of precious days that shine;
A glowing token of each lovely year
That you spent here upon the earth, mother dear.
Those years from birth, to marriage, to our father
Are known to us only from you, our mother.
As I write this story, each memory's sweet;
Like the ice cream and popsicles you gave to treat.
When I am discouraged, from my treasure chest
I count my golden coins. Like flowers pressed,
They breathe a fragrant memory of you,
Who wouldn't hesitate to change a shoe
For a view of the garden scene,
With blue delphiniums, red roses and peppers green,
Currants and berries to be harvested,
Or, carrots, beans and beets instead.
Like a miser, my seven-and-eighty coins I hold
Each one, dear mother, with you a year of gold.

(Barbara and James Cromwell)

Chapter 1

A Picture is Worth a Thousand Words

Imagine an area one hundred and fifty feet long and seventy-five feet wide surrounded by a fence seven and a half feet high. Let's peak inside and see the beautiful tabernacle. Deep red, blue, purple and gold colours shout out at you. The tabernacle is covered in curtains made of the finest linen in blue, purple and scarlet with cherubs, beautiful winged angels, embroidered all around. All the wood is covered in gold. Over a million dollars worth of gold and silver was used—many, many golden coins.

The tent covering the tabernacle was cloth made from goats' hair, then a covering of red leather made from the hide of rams, next a covering of badger skins. The tent was supported by a ridge-pole at the top.

In the courtyard stood a large bronze altar seven and a half feet square, four and a half feet high, for sacrificing animals. The fire was miraculously kindled and never went out. Also in the courtyard was a bronze washbasin for the priests to wash their hands and feet before ministering to God. See the beautiful garments the priests wore. The High Priest was spectacularly clad. The robe was a deep royal blue, so rich, with bells along the hem—everyone could hear the High Priest as he walked along. The cape covering the robe, called an ephod, was made of gold thread woven into blue, purple and scarlet fine linen. The breastplate was about ten inches square and it was a work of art to behold. Once again gold, blue, purple and scarlet were the brilliant colours of the fine linen. The breastplate was fastened with gold chains to the ephod. There were twelve brilliant sparkling stones—when the sun struck them the brilliant streaks of light burst out in rainbow hues. See the reds, blues, greens, turquoise, purple, yellow—all in settings of gold—golden coins and sparkling gems.

Inside the tabernacle the richness of gold was evident everywhere you looked. The table was made of acacia wood and covered with pure gold. It held ten loaves of bread with fresh ones placed on it once a week on the Sabbath.

The six branched candlestick stood five feet tall and was made of beaten gold. Olive oil was used to keep the candles burning brightly all the time. The Altar of Incense was three and a half feet high and one and a half feet square, made of acacia wood and overlaid with pure gold. Incense was burned on it morning and evening, a pleasing aroma to God. Then there was a curtain in front of the Most Holy Place where no priest dared go inside. The High Priest entered once a year. Inside was the most beautiful item of all—the Ark of the Covenant. It was a chest almost four feet long, over two feet high and over two feet wide. It was made of acacia wood completely covered with gold. The lid was of solid gold and two cherubim with their wings spread out faced each other. It was beautiful. Inside the Ark were the two tablets of stone on which the Ten Commandments were chiseled. When God chose Aaron's family to be His High Priests, he proved this to the Israelites by having Aaron's rod bud and produce almonds overnight! Aaron's rod was kept in the ark. God fed the Israelites with manna for forty years while they travelled in the Sinai Peninsula. Manna was like coriander seed and tasted like honey and wafers. A pot of manna was stored in the Ark of the Covenant.

The Levites served with the priests in the tabernacle. They camped around the tabernacle enclosure. To the north of the Levites were the camps for the tribes of Dan, Asher and Naphtali. To the west, Benjamin, Manasseh and Ephraim set up their tents. In the south were Gad, Simeon and Reuben. Judah, Issachar and Zebulon camped to the east. For forty years the Israelites wandered in the wilderness. Their clothes didn't wear out and their sandals didn't get holes in them for God provided for them.

They never knew how long they would be camping by the palm trees—when they were nicely settled into a routine, the trumpet would sound and they would pack up to move on. They were always leaving the familiar behind. Everything was strange for them from the time they left Egypt where they had grown up. For 400 years they had been slaves in Egypt. What a thrill to be free! But freedom had its many challenges too.

A pillar of cloud overshadowed them during the day time to protect them from the burning heat of the sun. At night it got so cold in the dessert that they were especially glad of the heat provided by the pillar of fire, as well as some welcome subdued light to break the pitch darkness of the night. The stars shone brilliantly from the heavens like coins of sparkling gold.

I was a leader at "Happy Hour" at York Road Baptist Church and I made a model of the tabernacle that Moses was directed by God to make when the children of Israel were in the wilderness. There were flannel graph pictures to go with the tabernacle model to teach the children the story.

The use of flannel boards for telling stories was a new thing in the 1950s. A board was covered with flannel and propped on an easel. Large colourful pictures of people and events in the stories were added to the board to illustrate the story being told.

The story of God creating the world was beautifully portrayed on the flannel board. When God decided to re-create the earth, it was dark and covered with water. The first day he created light which he called day, and the dark he called night. The second day he separated the waters above the earth (heaven) with the air in between the water over the earth. The next day he created dry land called the earth, and the water was the seas and oceans. Next he created the sun to provide light during the day, and the moon to reflect the sun's light at night, and the stars so that we would have days, months, seasons, and years. See the bright, colourful pictures on the flannel board as the story unfolds. Then the fish in the sea and the birds in the air were created. Can you see the fish swimming—the small ones, as well as the big whales and dolphins? Can you hear the birds singing—see the red cardinal, the robin with its cheery red breast, the blue jay, the bright orange of the Baltimore oriole? Next the grass, flowers, and trees were made—look at the variety, see the beautiful colours of the daffodils, tulips and hyacinths. Taste the ripe pear fresh from the tree. See the beautiful red cherries. Then God created the first man Adam, and out of his rib, God created the first woman, Eve. The Garden of Eden was a beautiful place to live. There was no smog, no pollution; the waters were clear and pure. The animals were tame, there was harmony in everything.

The story of Noah's Ark was another favourite on the flannel board. See the animals coming two-by-two to go into the ark—the elephants, giraffes, monkeys, lions, zebras, cats and dogs. What variety of animals there are on the earth.

The story of Hannah praying for a child and God answering with a little boy whom she named Samuel—feel the love of mother for her child. Hannah gave Samuel back to God to serve Him in the tabernacle. Each year she made a new little coat for her son. Each coat was a little bigger—can you picture those coats each year? Maybe the first year it was blue, the next year green. What's your favourite colour? Maybe Hannah made one of that colour one year. I wonder if Samuel was lonely and missed his Mommy.

The story of Joseph and his beautiful coat of many colours that his father made for him comes alive in vivid pictures. Daniel in the lion's den when God tamed the lions so that Daniel would not be harmed by them. See the sling shot that David is swinging as he approaches the huge giant named Goliath. The stone lands right in the centre of Goliath's forehead and he falls to the ground. The story of Moses seeing the burning bush and going up the mountainside to investigate—can you see that bush on fire? That's when God told Moses He was sending him to Egypt to bring his people out of slavery and into the Promised Land.

Even as God provided for the Israelites, He provided me with guidance and direction and comfort each day of my life. I had many times of loneliness and I turned to Him to fill the void. I had a song in my heart.

Like many people, I had a need to love and be loved and I pursued this throughout my lifetime. I looked for sunshine and warmth. Much of my life I was leaving the familiar behind and moving on to new challenges. When my pouch of gold coins was filling up, something would come along to take some of the sunshine away, but then there were new experiences to add more coins along the way. Searching for the meaning in life was a lifelong pursuit. I went through periods of loneliness and isolation, continually seeking for companionship, enjoying it while I had it, never knowing how long it would last. I had the great honour of being a mother to five children, to lead and direct them as they were growing up, and to watch them blossom into adults. During their young lives, finances were tight, but we were able to enjoy the small things in life knowing that some of the best things in life are free. Picnicking and swimming at the OR was free and only required making the lunch and walking to the lake to spend the day with the children, with several of the neighbourhood children tagging along.

Chapter 2

Four Leaf Clover

WEATHER

Whether the weather be fine
Or whether the weather be not,
Whether the weather be cold
Or whether the weather be hot,
We'll weather the weather
Whatever the weather,
Whether we like it or not.
 A saying my Mother repeated

Dad used to say, "That that is is. That that is not is not. Is not that so?"

Elizabeth Ellen Clayton (1878-1949) was born in Higher Openshaw near Manchester, in County of Lancashire, England on October 21.

Manchester was the world's first industrialized city and played a central role during the Industrial Revolution. It was the dominant international centre of textile manufacture and cotton spinning, thus being dubbed "Cottonopolis" and "Warehouse City" during the Victorian era with one hundred and eight cotton mills in 1853.

Engineering firms initially made machines for the cotton trade, but diversified into general manufacture. Similarly, the chemical industry started by producing bleaches and dyes, but expanded into other areas. Commerce was supported by financial service industries such as banking and insurance. Trade, and feeding the growing population, required a large transport and distribution infrastructure: the canal system was extended, and Manchester was at one end of the world's first intercity passenger railway—the Liverpool and Manchester Railway.

The Manchester Ship Canal was created by canalization of the Rivers Irwell and Mersey for thirty-six miles from Salford to the Mersey estuary. This enabled ocean going ships to sail right into the Port of Manchester.

Like most of the UK, the Manchester area mobilized extensively during World War II. Casting and machining expertise at Beyer, Peacock and Company's locomotive works in Gorton was switched to bomb making; Dunlop's rubber works in Chorlton-on-Medlock made barrage balloons; and in Trafford Park, engineers Metropolitan-Vickers made Avro Manchester and Avro Lancaster bombers and Ford built the Rolls-Royce Merlin engines to power them. Manchester was the target of bombing by the Luftwaffe, and by late 1940 air raids were taking place against non-military targets. The biggest took place during the "Christmas Blitz" on the nights of December 22 and 23, 1940, when an estimated 475 tons of high explosives plus over 37,000 incendiary bombs were dropped.

William Mann Todd (1889-1972) was born in Peterborough, County of Cambridge, England on November 14. He was 5'6" tall, had brown eyes and brown hair, and followed the Church of England religion.

Peterborough, a cathedral city seventy-five miles north of London, is situated on the River Nene, which flows into the North Sea. The local topography is flat and low-lying, and in some places below sea level. The Fens lie to the east of the city. Human settlement in the area dates back to the Bronze Age, and it was occupied by the Romans when it was an important area of ceramic production, providing Nene Valley Ware that was traded as far away as Cornwall. The Anglo-Saxon period saw the establishment of a monastery, which later became Peterborough Cathedral. The Peterborough Chronicle, which contains unique information about the history of England after the Norman Conquest, was composed here in the twelfth century by monks of the abbey. The population grew rapidly following the arrival of the railways in the nineteenth century, and Peterborough became an industrial centre, noted for the manufacture of bricks.

After 1910, Elizabeth and William immigrated to Canada with their families and it was in Canada where they met. They were married on August 25, 1913 in St. George's Cathedral, Kingston, Ontario.

The following year, William took his wife to visit his family in England. While there, Emma was born on April 20, 1914 at 20 Rivett Street, West Ham. Emma died shortly after returning to Canada on July 30, 1914 and was buried in St. John's Cemetery in Toronto. Their second child was a son, William Joseph, born on September 14, 1915 in Kingston, Ontario.

I was born on February 23, 1920 at 36 James Street, Kingston and given the name May Todd. Kingston is a city located at the eastern end of Lake Ontario, where the lake runs into the St. Lawrence River and the Thousand Islands begin. Kingston is nicknamed the "Limestone City" because of the many historic buildings built from the local limestone, a sedimentary rock composed largely of the mineral calcite.

Kingston's location at the Rideau Canal entrance to Lake Ontario, after canal construction was completed in 1832, made it the primary military and economic centre of Upper Canada. Kingston had the largest population of any centre in Upper Canada until the 1840s and was chosen as the first capital of the united Canadas, serving in that role from 1841 to 1844, with the first meeting of Parliament on June 13, 1841 being held on the site of what is now Kingston General Hospital. Kingston's location made it vulnerable to American attack, resulting in the capital being moved to alternating locations in Montreal and Toronto, and later to Ottawa in 1857. Kingston was the home of Canada's first Prime Minister, Sir John A. Macdonald.

In the year 1920, the population of the world was 1,811,000,000. The 19th amendment has just given American women the vote. Ireland had been partitioned and the six northern counties remained part of the United Kingdom. Time Magazine was launched. Prime Minister Borden resigned and Arthur Meighen was sworn in as the new Prime Minister of Canada. Passing an English literacy test became a prerequisite to immigrate into Canada. The Royal Northwest Mounted Police merged with the Dominion police force to form the Royal Canadian Mounted Police. Women's hemlines were escalating and were astonishingly nearer the knee than the ankle. The Group of Seven paintings were exhibited for the first time in Toronto.

We moved to Belleville, Ontario when I was small. Belleville, a French word meaning "beautiful city," is located at the mouth of the Moira River on the Bay of Quinte in southeastern Ontario. Procter & Gamble, Kellogg's, Lipton, Wilson Sports, Sears and Nortel are among the internationally known companies with industrial operations in Belleville. The central Canadian Forces Post Office (CFPO) is located here, the mailing address for Canadian Armed Forces Bases and Ships abroad.

We lived first on Station Street, then at 350 Bleecker Avenue. Milk was delivered to our front door-step from a horse-drawn van. The house on Bleecker Avenue had three big rooms downstairs—kitchen, dining room and living room. There was a large clock on the wall in the kitchen with Roman numerals on it.

The Romans were active in trade and commerce, and from the time of learning to write they needed a way to indicate numbers. The system they developed lasted many centuries, and still sees some specialized use today. Roman numerals traditionally indicate the order of rulers or ships who share the same name (i.e. Queen Elizabeth II). The big differences between Roman and Arabic numerals (the ones we use today) are that Romans didn't have a symbol for zero, and numeral placement within a number can indicate subtraction rather than addition. The easiest way to note down a number is to make that many marks—little I's. Thus I means 1, II means 2, III means 3. However, four strokes seemed like too many so the Romans moved on to the symbol 5-V. Placing I in front of the V—or placing any smaller number in front of any larger number—indicated subtraction. So IV means 4. After V comes a series of additions—VI means 6, VII means 7, VIII means 8. X means 10 . . . but wait—what about 9? Same deal—IX means to subtract I from X, leaving 9. Numbers in the teens, twenties and thirties follow the same form as the first set, only with X's indicating the number of tens. So XXXI is 31, and XXIV is 24. L means 50, C stands for *centum*, the Latin word for 100. A centurion led 100 men. We still use this in words like "century" and "cent".

A door off the dining room led through a hall to the front door. A telephone hung on the wall—much different than the ones we see today.

The ability to communicate over distance is part of human history. The earliest primitive methods such as beating drums led to the use of smoke signals, beacons of light and flags. An electrical telegraph was developed and patented in the United States in 1837 by Samuel F. B. Morse revolutionizing long distance communication.

Alexander Graham Bell gave the world a number of time-saving, life-changing inventions that continue to make our lives easier. It was Bell's interest in improving the lives of the deaf that motivated many of his inventions in the telecommunication field. Communication always played a large role in the Scottish physicist's life as his father was a speech pathologist and taught him about speech impediments and dealing with the issues of the deaf community. The fact that Mrs. Bell, Alexander's mother was deaf was a motivating factor for both father and son.

In 1872, Alexander moved to America to teach at the Boston School for the Deaf, where he focused his time on teaching his hard of hearing students to speak, a very new concept. Sound, speech and hearing constantly consumed Bell's mind and life. Bell married one of his students, Mabel Hubbard.

Bell hoped to improve on the telegraph by finding a way to get messages from one telegraph station to another without them having to be taken on foot. He hoped to use tonal noises sent by wire between stations to communicate the text of messages. He was working on this invention when he met another famous inventor, Thomas Watson. Watson worked in an electric shop in which he was often assigned to assist inventors with their ideas. When working with Bell, the two accidentally transmitted sound through wire using electromagnets. The concept of the telephone was born.

In 1876 at the age of 29, Alexander Graham Bell was given a patent for the first operational telephone. The first conversation to take place over the wire systems occurred on March 10 of that year when Mr. Bell called Mr. Watson to assist him with some spilled battery acid. Watson clearly heard Bell's voice travel through the wires and came to his assistance. It was this invention that changed the way people communicate throughout the world.

Bell always considered himself a teacher and not an inventor. His work with deaf students inspired others, including the famous Helen Keller who dedicated her own biography to him. Today we remember Bell as the inventor of the telephone and forget the steps that lead him to that discovery and the people who inspired his work. Imagining a world without his work is difficult with the telephone being as ubiquitous as the television set or the refrigerator. Inventions become essential to civilization over time and it is hard to imagine there was a time when they didn't exist.

A stairway off the kitchen led up to two bedrooms at the back of the house and also a smaller room containing the toilet, with a window overlooking the school that I attended.

Before mechanical refrigeration systems were introduced, people cooled their food with ice and snow, either found locally or brought down from the mountains. The first cellars were holes dug into the ground and lined with wood or straw and packed with snow and ice: this was the only means of refrigeration for most of history. In our kitchen was a door to a good-sized pantry with shelves and cupboards for food. There was a trap door in the floor of the pantry, with a ladder leading down to the partially dug-out basement with a dirt floor. Dad made shelves and Mom kept her preserves and pickles on them. She stored eggs in a large crock, and root crops such as potatoes, carrots, turnips, beets and parsnips.

In order to help fresh food last longer, an efficient method of keeping the produce cool enough had to be created. Inventors worked for years to create an efficient icebox. Iceboxes work best with a proper balance of insulation and air circulation.

In 1803, Maryland native Thomas Moore patented the first "refrigerator", which greatly changed the agricultural business. Thomas lived on a farm twenty miles outside the city of Washington, with the village of Georgetown as the market center. Moore devised an icebox out of a cedar tub which was insulated with rabbit fur, filled with ice, and wrapped in a piece of sheet metal so he could transport his butter to market at a cooler temperature. In the warmer months of the year, Moore noticed that people would pass up his competitors' butter, which had softened up or melted, for his butter which was wrapped up and came in individual bricks.

With the invention of the icebox, the ice industry developed. In the eighteenth century, wealthy people used ice for cooling beverages and making ice cream. Each winter, men went out onto lakes and cut larges slabs of ice and stored them in underground icehouses for future use. The ice cutter was created to make cutting ice from the lakes easier; the above ground icehouse provided cheaper access to ice and more farmers and households became interested in refrigeration. Farmers were able to offer a wider range of goods to sell as well as travel further with them, increasing their scope of sales. Items that were not previously marketable without refrigeration, such as fresh meat and dairy products, (with cheese and butter being an exception) were now profitable. With refrigeration, food could be stored longer, thus eliminating the need for daily trips to the market.

In the early 1900's companies like Frigidaire and Maytag began marketing electric refrigerators for home use. In the beginning, these were used seasonally, primarily by upper class citizens. Compared to an icebox, an electric fridge was extremely expensive to run, not to mention the costs of getting a DC outlet installed in the home.

There was a space, just inside the door of our pantry, for an icebox. Blocks of ice were stored in the top of the icebox so cold air would circulate downwards to keep the food cool. The iceman would bring a big block of ice to put in it. He used large black iron tongs to grip the block and carry it to the icebox. The tongs weighed as much as the block of ice! Children would hang around waiting to pick up small pieces of ice that he sometimes chipped off with an ice pick. We would suck on these refreshing ice chips, a real treat on a hot summer afternoon. As the ice melted in the icebox, a small tube carried the water to a pan, which sat on the floor underneath. The pan had to be emptied several times a day, depending on the season. In the winter we would get away with emptying it morning and night, but in the summer, it had to be emptied more often. On a bitterly cold winter night if the ice pan overflowed, there would be a good coating of ice covering the floor in the kitchen the next morning. The ice didn't melt until long after Dad got a roaring fire going in the stove.

Mom and Dad slept in the smallest bedroom, while my brother and I shared the larger one while I was small. Later, I was given my parent's room and they slept in the living room on a new chesterfield which opened into a bed. A door separated us from three more upstairs rooms which were rented to a widow named Mrs. Kent, her son, Cyril, and daughter, Lillian.

We had a very large garden where Dad grew all kinds of flowers and vegetables. I remember his beautiful dahlias in a rainbow of colours, and the lovely large, fragrant, creamy-white flowers on the Yucca-filamentosa which is commonly called Adam's Needle. Dad was especially proud of his beefsteak tomatoes and would send me to Ainsworth's store on the corner of Bleecker Avenue and Pine Street, two doors away from our house, to get them weighed. They were big! Dad worked in his garden until late in the evenings. It was so dark Mom wondered how he could see to do anything. Whenever he planned to go fishing, he would be out there the night before collecting worms and putting them in a can to use as bait.

In our backyard we had White Leghorn chickens. Leghorns are one of the best known breeds of chicken and produce the majority of the world's crop of white eggs. Dad built the chicken coop which my brother had to clean every week. I remember helping him one time but I didn't like the smell! Mom cooked the vegetable peelings and scraps from the table, in a big pot. She fed it to the chickens along with corn which she scattered into the fenced-in chicken run.

Mr. Morgan was a friend who was often invited to our home for Sunday supper. When I was a young girl, he bought me a set of dishes. Other friends of Mom and Dad who came to visit us were the Tom Ellertons', the Bamfords', the Jim Hearsts' and the Marshs' families from Kingston. I remember two daughters, Annie and Edith Bamford, who were looking in the lawn for a three leaf clover. I found a six leaf clover and one of the girls pulled three leaves off, told me not to tell, and said she had found a three leaf clover. I don't know if anyone guessed what she had done. The laugh was on the girls! The four-leaf clover is an uncommon variation of the common, three-leaved clover. According to tradition, such leaves bring good luck to their finders, especially if found accidentally. According to legend, each leaflet represents something: the first is for hope, the second is for faith, the third is for love, and the fourth is for luck. It has been estimated that there are approximately 10,000 three-leaf clovers for every four-leaf clover.

One time when we travelled to Kingston to visit friends, our car went out of control. We were coming around a big curve on the highway and the car headed straight across the road in front of oncoming traffic. They could see Dad was frantically turning the wheel but the car did not respond. We just missed the edge of a cement culvert as the car went down into the ditch and halfway up the other side, where it came to rest, tilted at an angle. None of us were hurt but Dad had to hitchhike to the nearest town, Deseronto, to buy a new tire. We sat on the grass by the roadside until Dad got back. Just before our trip the car had been overhauled but someone had not properly tightened up a nut. Dad was very angry with the negligent person because we could have been killed if the car had hit the culvert. We eventually arrived in Kingston, but coming home that night the car ran out of gas. Dad had filled the tank before leaving in the morning so there should have been plenty. However, he hadn't realized that while the car was tilted in the ditch the gas was leaking out. Poor Dad had to walk again, this time to the nearest gas station to bring back a can of gas.

Dad built a garage in the backyard for his first car, a Ford. He had to crank the car to get the motor going. One time I got behind the wheel to help him. Dad said to me, "When I turn the crank and you hear the motor start pull the choke to keep it going." Sometimes it wouldn't work with the first crank, so Dad had to keep cranking. That was really hard work. Later he had a newer model that started by putting your foot on a pedal on the floor.

The first Model T Ford was built in 1908. It had the steering wheel on the left, which every other company soon copied. The entire engine and transmission were enclosed; the four cylinders were cast in a solid block; the suspension used two semi-elliptic springs.

The car was very simple to drive, easy and cheap to repair. It was so cheap at $825 in 1908 (the price fell every year—by 1916 the price dropped to $360 for the basic touring car. Using the Consumer Price Index, this price was equivalent to $7,020 in 2008 dollars).

Ford created a massive publicity machine in Detroit to ensure every newspaper carried stories and ads about the new product. Ford's network of local dealers made the car ubiquitous with it turning up in every city in North America. As independent dealers, the franchises grew rich and publicized not just the Ford but the very concept of automobiling; local motor clubs sprang up to help new drivers to explore the countryside. Farmers looked on the vehicle as a commercial device to help their business. In 1913 Ford introduced the moving assembly belts into his plants, enabling a huge increase in production.

By 1918, half of all cars in America were Model T's. Until the development of the assembly line, which mandated black because of its quicker drying time, Model T's were available in other colors including red. American drivers learned on the Model T. In December 1927 the Model A Ford was introduced.

Dad used his bicycle for travelling part of the way to work. He parked his bicycle and got a ride by truck to Corbyville distillery about five miles away. He worked in the plant, and also maintained the lawn and garden. Before that he had worked in a shoe factory.

On the early Ontario frontier, whisky was likely to be as much a part of daily life as bread and meat. Two of the most famous names in Canadian distilling got their start in the business as baker and cattleman. Henry Corby, of French Huguenot stock, learned the baking trade in London, England, before emigrating at age 26 to Canada where he set up a small food shop and bakery in Belleville in 1832. After service during the 1837 Rebellion, he sold his bakery and bought a St. Lawrence steamer, the "Queen", which he operated for four years buying and selling grain.

In 1857 he built a grist-mill on the banks of the Moira River with its clear sparkling iron-free water. Farmers brought their grain to be ground into meal, reserving a portion to be made into whisky. Henry Corby became interested in the distilling process, making his own brand of whisky for local consumption; by 1859 the distillery was equal in importance to the mill.

The same year Henry Corby opened his mill on the Moira, J. P. Wiser came to Canada from Upper New York State with a dream of becoming a cattle baron. He built facilities for fattening 2,000 head of cattle. He managed a distillery next door and fed the cattle on the spent grain from the distillery, which by the late 1860's was processing 900 bushels of grain a day during the distilling season.

The American War between the States created a great demand for both meat and whisky, and both Wiser enterprises flourished. By 1884, his oldest son Harlow was overseeing operations on J. P's 150,000 acre cattle ranch in Kansas and sending cattle back to Ontario to be fattened at the distillery before being shipped to markets in Britain.

The name Wiser gained a reputation for quality whisky and the cattle business soon became secondary to the distillery, a full-scale operation that demanded the services of skilled craftsmen and workmen from all over Upper Canada. Coopers, carpenters, teamsters, master blenders, dock workers and others all found employment at J.P. Wiser's distillery. Shortly after World War I ended, Corby's and Wiser's distilleries joined forces.

Christmas or plum pudding, the dessert traditionally served on Christmas day, is a steamed pudding with dried fruit and nuts, usually made with suet, and is very dark in appearance as a result of the dark sugars and black molasses, as well as its long cooking time. Every year Mom made plum puddings. It was common practice to include small silver coins in the pudding mixture, which could be kept by the person whose serving included them. The usual choice was a silver three pence or sixpence. The coin was believed to bring wealth in the coming year. Other tokens also known to have been included were a tiny wishbone (to bring good luck), a silver thimble (for thrift), or an anchor (to symbolize safe harbour). Dad used to say things and get us really excited every time we took a bite. As young children eating those puddings was a thrilling experience and we each hoped to be the lucky one to find the sixpence. Of course, the addition of the surprise in the pudding also encouraged us to eat our pudding.

Sixpences have been seen as a lucky charm for brides. An old rhyme, "Something old, something new, something borrowed, something blue, and a sixpence for her shoe." The folk song "I've Got Sixpence" was written of this coin.

The singer tells the tale of spending two pence (per verse) until he has "no pence to send home to my wife—poor wife." In Elizabethan times, the sixpence was roughly a day's wage for rustic labour in the provinces. With it, you could buy two dinners.

Dad used to take us in the car to lake or river areas where the fishing was good, fishing mainly for bass. Sometimes Dad and my brother would take a boat out on the lake and fish for hours. Mom and I would sit under a tree and I would also play in the water near the shore. Mom always liked being by the water. I enjoyed the picnic lunches that Mom made. She took jars of preserved fruit, brown sugar tarts, butter in a jar, sliced bread for sandwiches, made fresh right at the picnic site. I remember going to Frankford on the Bay of Quinte several times; the water there was lovely and clear. We always liked it when Dad went home by way of Corbyville where he worked because he would go in and get us an ice cream cone.

One summer my Grandfather, Joseph Clayton, Aunt Evelyn, Uncle Lem and their six children came from New Liskeard, Ontario, to spend a holiday with us in Belleville. It was very exciting having so many people in our home. I can remember beds and cots all over the place. This was Mom's father, and Mom's sister and her family. My brother, my cousins and I found a spring somewhere off Pine Street and we took bottles and jars to fill with this beautiful cold water—the drink of choice for thirst in those days with pop being a luxury that was enjoyed on rare occasions. I liked Canada Dry Ginger Ale and Orange Crush when I could have it.

Our family went by train from Belleville to Toronto to visit the Canadian National Exhibition (CNE). In those days the manufacturers gave away lots of free samples; we would come home with two or three shopping bags full of various kinds of chocolate bars, candies, toffee, school supplies, and other items. There were many samples of different foods that you could eat right on the premises.

The CNE, founded in 1879, is an 18-day fair held every August until Labour Day on one hundred and ninety-two acres of land at Exhibition Place in Toronto. Its roots are in agriculture, featuring a working farm and a horse show. Central to any fair is its midway with rides and games for the young and the not so young. What would a fair be without cotton candy and candy apples?

In 1879, general admission was 25 cents and more than 100,000 people attended. At the first Canadian National Exhibition, fair-goers arrived in horse-drawn carriages, on bicycles, by railway or steamship, with the automobile still in its infancy. In 1897, the CNE brought the automobile to the Canadian public in exhibits that were for many their first encounter with this marvel of engineering. Automobile shows were popular attractions, leading to the development of the Automotive Building in 1929.

Exhibits feature the latest technological advances in industry and agriculture. CNE patrons were introduced to electric railway transportation in 1883, to Edison's phonograph in 1888, to the wireless telephone in the 1890s, to radio in 1922, to television in 1939, and to plastics and synthetics in the 1940s and 1950s.

From 1942 until the end of the war, the facilities at Exhibition Park were used for barracks for the soldiers as part of the war effort. Today, the military tradition continues at the CNE with the annual Warriors' Day Parade held on the first Saturday of each Exhibition.

When Mom was preparing a turkey for the oven one day, she was plucking the feathers and cleaning it, using a big pan of hot water on the table. She fell and the water went all over the floor and Mom was sitting in it. She called me to drag her out of the hot water. A neighbour who was a nurse came over to see Mom and told her she had had a stroke. Perhaps as a result of Mom's high blood pressure, a blood vessel had ruptured in her brain and caused the stroke. It was a little scary for me, but being just ten years old I didn't really understand how serious this could have been.

Chapter 3

Bullets, Bullets Everywhere

Dad was mobilized for active service in the First World War with the 14th Regiment (Prince of Wales Own Rifles) with the Canadian Armed Forces in Kingston on October 25, 1914 and saw service in Canada, Britain and France.

4th CMR was raised in Toronto, Ontario with the assignment 2nd Canadian Mounted Rifles Brigade in December 1915. In January 1916, they were brigaded as part of the 8th Canadian Brigade into the Third Infantry Division in the Canada Corps. The 4th C.M.R. was a battalion of a thousand men, representing six hundred and fifty fighting men.

The Canadian Corps was commanded by British Lieutenant General E. A. H. Alderson until 1916 when another British Lieutenant General Julia Byng took over. When Byng was promoted to an Army command, he was succeeded in June 1917 by the commander of the 1st Division, General Arthur W. Currie, giving the corps its first Canadian commander.

William Mann Todd D.C.M. Reg. No. 835512, 4.C.M.R.R. fought in Battles: Vimy Ridge April 9, 1917; Passchendaele October 26, 1917; Amiens August 8, 1918; Arras August 26 and 28, 1918.

The capture of Vimy Ridge symbolized Canada's significant achievements during the war. As part of a British offensive around Arras in April 1917, the Canadian Corps was to seize heavily-fortified Vimy Ridge in northern France. The Canadians carefully planned and rehearsed their attack. In the week leading up to the battle, Canadian and British artillery pounded the enemy positions on the ridge, killing and tormenting defenders. New artillery tactics allowed the gunners to first target, then destroy enemy positions.

A nearly limitless supply of artillery shells and the new 106 fuse, which allowed shells to explode on contact, as opposed to burying themselves in ground, facilitated the destruction of hardened defenses and barbed wire. The Canadian infantry were well supported when it went into battle with over 1,000 artillery pieces laying down withering, supportive fire. At 5:30 on the morning of 9 April, 1917, all four Canadian divisions, advancing together for the first time, stormed the seven-kilometre-long ridge and captured it, with two remaining German positions falling three days later. The cost to Canada was high: 3,598 killed and over 7,000 wounded. But the Canadians' determination earned them a reputation as formidable, effective troops. Vimy became a symbol for the sacrifice of the young Dominion.

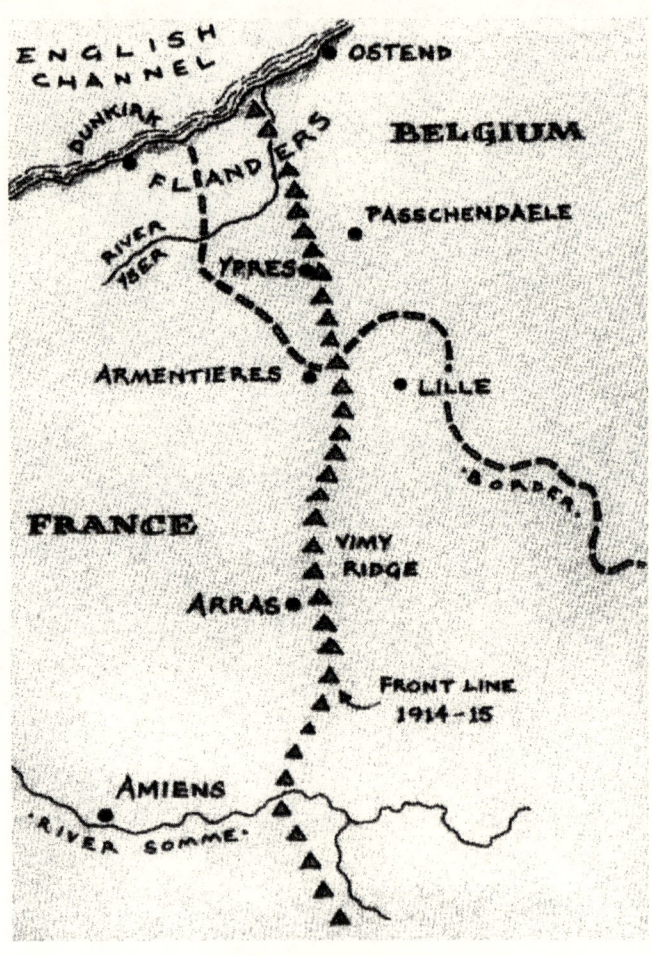

The Canadian Corps played a leading role in achieving Allied victory. In October and November 1917, fighting on horrific battlefields in waist-deep mud, the Corps captured Passchendaele, in Belgium. Passchendaele, the 3rd Battle of Ypres, was one of the most controversial battles of the entire war. Situated in a low-lying area reclaimed from marshy lands by means of an elaborate drainage system, the vulnerable terrain was easily and quickly destroyed by shellfire; once shelling started, flooding rapidly turned the whole battlefield into a sea of mud. To add to the misery, Flanders was notorious for wet weather, which usually started in the late fall. Canadian troops took over operations at Passchendaele on October 26 and extended British efforts that yielded an advance of only nine kilometers on the Allied front and did not succeed in meeting the ultimate objective for the battle—breaking through German lines and freeing Belgian ports of the German U-boat menace.

The Battle of Amiens began on August 8, 1918 and was the opening phase of the Allied offensive. On March 21, 1918, Germany had launched Operation Michael, the first of a series of attacks that would drive the Allies back along the length of the Western Front. Michael itself was aimed at the town of Amiens, a vital railway junction, but the advance had been halted at Villers-Bretonneux by the Australians on April 4. Subsequent German offensives, Operation Georgette (April 9-11), Operation Blucher-Yorck (May 27), Operation Gneisenau (June 9) and Operation Marne-Rheims (July 15-17), had made advances but failed to achieve a decisive breakthrough.

When the Marne-Rheims offensive petered out, the Allied supreme commander, French Field Marshal Ferdinand Foch, ordered a counter-offensive which became the Second Battle of the Marne. The Germans withdrew from the Marne to the north.

The Somme was chosen as a suitable site for the next offensive action. The initial attack was to be made by the British Fourth Army, commanded by General Sir Henry Rawlinson. The massed artillery would open fire at zero hour, at the same time as the infantry advanced. The movement and assembly of tanks were drowned out by low flying aircraft. The British had concentrated 324 Mark IV and Mark V battle tanks, 184 supply tanks and two battalions of light (14 ton) Medium Mark A "Whippet" tanks.

An elaborate deception was carried out to make the Germans believe the veteran Canadian Corps were elsewhere. A Canadian unit made itself obvious at Ypres and faked radio signals were used to suggest the corps was near Calais. The corps was secretly transported from Arras and was in position east of Amiens without the Germans being aware.

The battle began in dense fog at 4:20 a.m. on August 8. From north to south the attacking formations of the Fourth Army were the British III Corps (north of the Somme), the Australian Corps and the Canadian Corps. The French First Army would keep contact in the south before making its own attack later.

In the first phase seven divisions attacked, with the aim being to capture the first German position, advancing about 4000 yards, an objective they reached by 7:30 a.m. In the centre, the leading divisions had been followed up by supporting units who would move through to attack the second objective a further two miles distant. While the infantry were still short of the second objective, sixteen armoured cars broke through towards Peronne and proceeded to roam the German rear, causing panic and confusion.

By the end of the advance, a gap fifteen miles long had been punched in the German line south of the Somme. Total German losses were estimated to be 30,000 on August 8 while the Allies suffered about 6,500 killed, wounded and missing.

The advance continued for three more days but without the spectacular results of August 8 as the rapid progress had outrun the supporting artillery. On August 10 there were signs that the Germans were pulling out.

The German commander-in-chief, General Erich Ludendorff, described August 8, 1918 as "the black day of the German Army", not because of the ground lost to the advancing Allies but because the morale of the German troops had sunk to the point where large scale capitulations occurred.

By succeeding in destroying the very heart of the German defense system, the Canadians enabled the British 3rd Army to advance eastward at a great pace. The success of the 2nd Battle of Arras, August 26-September 3, 1918, had a positive effect all along the western front, presaging an imminent Allied victory.

After the Allied success in the Battle of Amiens, August 8-11, it was expected that the enemy forces would be severely exhausted. "If we let the enemy rest," said Sir Douglas Haig, Commander-in-chief of the British Army, "it will regain its confidence and we will have to start using attrition tactics again." A renewal of the offensive on an extended front thus brought the Canadians back into action.

The British 1st Army was ordered to strike eastward from Arras, and the Canadian Corps, under the command of General Sir Arthur Currie, became the spearhead of the attack, as it had been in earlier battles.

The Canadians were on the Arras-Cambrai Road, with the Scarpe on their left, opposite a series of enemy defensive positions that were afforded good protection by the topography of the region. The battle zone extended northeast beyond the high Artois Hills. About 14 kilometres east of Arras was the Drocourt-Queant Line, an impressive, well-fortified system of trenches and shelters. This line of defense was designed to keep the Allies from advancing into the Douai Plain.

These positions were the initial objective of the Canadians. Since the enemy was expecting an attack, it was obviously impossible to surprise the Germans. The strategy adopted was to launch successive frontal attacks to exhaust the enemy troops.

General Currie had fourteen field artillery brigades and nine heavy artillery brigades at his disposal in the way of supporting fire. The massive artillery support proved to be crucial in advancing rapidly and exhausting enemy forces that were so well located in their defensive positions.

Monday, August 26 was chosen as the day of attack. The drizzling rain did not make the advance easy. H-hour [the time of day at which the military operation is scheduled to begin, from H (for hour) + hour], initially set for dawn, was moved up to 3:00 a.m. in the hopes of deceiving the enemy. The ruse worked as the surprised German soldiers put up little resistance and the Canadian infantry was able to progress quickly in the first moments of battle, without having to use armoured equipment.

The first objective was to capture a north-south line, west of Monchy-le-Preux, and then move east as far as possible. The intermediate objective was to break the Fresnes-Rouvroy Line and capture Cagnicourt, Dury and Etaing.

Once these maneuvers were successfully executed, an even larger task awaited the Canadians—breaking the Drocourt-Queant Line and, finally, establishing a front line immediately west of Canal-du-Nord, beyond which the enemy would likely have retreated.

On August 23, the Canadians raided the German-occupied city of Neuville-Vitasse in broad daylight and partially captured it. The enemy decided not to organize an extended defense when it realized that it was dealing with Canadians, whom it regarded as the best troops.

While the first objectives were being reached and the attack on the Drocourt-Queant Line was being planned, the major task was repairing and extending the roads and local railway lines, crucial for supplying the troops.

In the first three days of the battle, the 2nd and 3rd Division had advanced more than eight kilometers over rough, broken land furrowed with extremely well-fortified trenches. The Canadians succeeded in reaching the great majority of their objectives and captured 3,300 prisoners and a large number of guns.

From August 8, 1918 to the Armistice of November 11, the Canadians were in the forefront of the Allied advance that finally defeated Germany. The Corps had advanced as far as Mons, Belgium when the war ended.

William Mann Todd was given an Honourable Discharge on May 17, 1919 in Kingston, Ontario at the age of 30. All the soldiers received a British War Medal and a Victory Medal. Todd rescued a tank crew and dressed their wounds, and for his bravery won the Distinguished Conduct Medal (D.C.M.). During the war he was wounded in the right thigh which caused a limp for the remainder of his life and earned him a pension.

> "Private W. Todd, 4th Battalion, Canadian Mounted Rifle Regiment—For conspicuous gallantry and devotion to duty during the action on 9th August, 1918, near Folies. When acting as stretcher bearer with his platoon during the advance a Tank, which had been hit and had caught fire, he, on his own initiative and without assistance, rescued the crew from the burning tank. They were all wounded, and he dressed their wounds and got them to a place of safety, calling to a carrying party to remove them. He then rejoined his platoon and carried on with them throughout the action"—London Gazette

In 1922, the French government ceded to Canada in perpetuity Vimy Ridge, and the land surrounding it. The gleaming white marble and haunting sculptures of the Vimy Memorial stand as a terrible and poignant reminder of the Canadians who died serving their country during the First World War. At the base of the Memorial, these words appear in French and in English:

> To the valour of their countrymen in the Great War and in memory of their sixty thousand dead this monument is raised by the people of Canada

Designed by Canadian sculptor and architect Walter Seymour Allward, the monument rests on a bed of 11,000 tonnes of concrete, reinforced with hundreds of tonnes of steel. The towering pylons and sculptured figures contain 6,000 tonnes of limestone brought to the site from an abandoned Roman quarry on the Adriatic Sea. The figures were carved where they now stand from huge blocks of this stone. A cloaked figure stands at the front, or east side, of the monument overlooking the Douai Plain. It was carved from a single, 30-tonne block and is the largest piece in the monument. This sorrowing figure of a woman represents Canada—a young nation mourning her dead. Below is a tomb, draped in laurel branches and bearing a helmet and sword.

Carved on the walls of the monument are the names of 11,285 Canadian soldiers who were killed in France and whose final resting place was then unknown. Imagine how many hours it took to chisel all those names in the marble, a much bigger job than chiseling the Ten Commandments into the two stone tablets that Moses was charged with doing. Standing on the monument's wide stone terrace overlooking the broad fields and rolling hills of Northern France, one can see other places where Canadians fought and died. More than 66,000 Canadian service personnel died in the First World War.

The Memorial marks the site of the engagement that Canadians were to remember with more pride than any other operation of the First World War. It stands as a tribute to all who served their country in battle in that four-year struggle and particularly to those who gave their lives. The Vimy Ridge War Memorial took eleven years and $1.5 million to build and was unveiled on July 26, 1936 by King Edward VIII, in the presence of President Albert Lebrun of France and 50,000 or more Canadian and French veterans and their families, including William Mann Todd, his wife Elizabeth and their son William Joseph who travelled from England to France for the occasion.

As an important cultural resource located on a significant historic site, the restoration of the Canadian National Vimy Memorial presented unique technical challenges. The history of the monument's construction and the vision of its creator guided the restoration team in carrying out the work with particular care and craftsmanship. Restoration of the Canadian National Vimy Memorial took place over a two-year period and was completed in 2007. The work included dismantling and rebuilding stone structures in the monument's platform and vertical walls, replacing and re-engraving damaged stone, repointing the two massive pylons, cleaning the twenty statues that adorn the monument, and improving the drainage and lighting systems.

Chapter 4

School Days

At age 6 I began attending Queen Victoria School on Pine Street. The girls entrance faced Lingham Street, which was only a few minutes walk away from home. The subjects taught were Phonics, Reading, writing, arithmetic, Spelling, Literature and Composition, Grammar, Geography, Canadian History, British History, Art, Physical Education, Music.

Both Willie and I sang in the school choir; I was an alto. Tom Carruthers taught us our school song.

A contest was held for the school children to make posters and scrapbooks. Miss Myrtle Peck, a teacher at the school, chose Betty Pigden and myself to participate. We went to Miss Peck's home one evening to work on the projects. My poster had a sign: "DANGER, THIN ICE." The other project was making scrapbooks—I don't remember what they were about, but we glued pictures on the pages.

A woman's group called the Women's Christian Temperance Union, WCTU, came to our school to present prizes. On awards day with everyone in the auditorium, the women from WCTU on the stage called out the names of the winners. My name was called—I was at the back of the auditorium and had to go all the way to the front. Betty Pidgen won first prize and I won second for our scrapbooks. I just got back to my seat and my name was called again. I won first prize for my poster. I had to go all the way back up again! But it was worth it! I won a total of $4.00! That was a lot of money in the Depression Days. I put the money into my bank account, having learned the value of saving at a young age.

The WCTU talked to us about not drinking and students signed pledge cards that they would not drink. The WCTU was introduced in Canada in 1874 in Owen Sound, Ontario, and by 1883 it was active in every Canadian province.

The evangelistic group, The Women's Christian Temperance Union was the driving force behind Prohibition, an attempt to forbid by law the selling and drinking of intoxicating beverages. Prohibition was enacted in Prince Edward Island in 1901 and in the remaining provinces, the Yukon and Newfoundland during the First World War. The Canadian government controlled the making and trading of liquor and in March 1918 it stopped, for the duration of the war, the manufacture and importation of liquor into provinces where purchase was illegal. The aim was to close all drinking establishments, viewed as places of drunkenness and misery.

The provincial Temperance Acts closed legal drinking establishments and forbade the sale of alcohol for beverage purposes, and its possession and consumption except in a private dwelling. Alcohol could be purchased through government dispensaries for industrial, scientific, mechanical, artistic, sacramental and medicinal uses. Distillers and brewers properly licensed could sell outside the province. Although enforcement was difficult, drunkenness and associated crimes declined significantly. However, illicit stills and home-brewed "moonshine" increased.

As time progressed, the WCTU realized they could not stop people from drinking entirely and temperance advocates successfully pressured all provincial and territorial governments to curtail the sale of liquor through the tight control of liquor control boards. The fight against "demon rum" was connected to other reforms of the time, such as the women's suffrage movement for women to be able to vote in elections, and it was motivated in part by social gospel sentiment, an attempt to apply Christianity to the collective ills of an industrializing society.

Between 1920 and 1930, all the provinces, except Prince Edward Island, voted to end prohibition. PEI held out until 1948.

In 1932 we moved to a house on Markham Road in Malvern, Ontario, north east of Toronto. Dad's brother, Jack, and his family lived there.

I attended S.S. #6 School for two years. Having to walk one and a quarter miles each way was a new experience for me. There were no school buses in those days. In winter time it was quite a challenge. I also had to get used to eating sandwiches for lunch instead of a hot meal. The school had two rooms with one teacher looking after the younger children and Miss Young taught the older classes.

I remember the story our teacher read to us each morning, a chapter each day, called "The Secret Garden". Miss Young was one of the nicest teachers I ever had. After leaving Malvern in 1935, I continued to write letters to her for at least four years.

The Secret Garden by Frances Hodgson Burnett is about Mary Lennox, a sickly, sour-faced little girl born in India to wealthy British parents who showed little interest in her, leaving her in the care of an Ayah from birth. Orphaned by an outbreak of cholera, she is sent back to England to the legal guardianship of her only remaining relative, her father's brother-in-law, Archibald Craven, a reclusive widower. Craven is still mourning his wife, Lilias, who died ten years before. To escape his sad memories, he constantly travels abroad, leaving Mary and the manor under the supervision of his housekeeper, Mrs. Medlock. The only person who has any time for the little girl is the chambermaid Martha Sowerby, who tells Mary about a walled garden that was the late Mrs. Craven's favorite place. No one has entered the garden since she died because Archibald locked its entrance and buried the key.

Mary finds the key to the secret garden and a robin shows her where the door is hidden beneath overgrown ivy. Once inside, she discovers that although the roses seem lifeless, some of the other flowers have survived. She resolves to tend the garden herself. She recruits Martha's brother Dickon, who has a way with plants and wild animals, to help her. Dickon shows Mary that the roses are not dead. Thanks to her new-found interests and activities, Mary begins to blossom, losing her sickly look and unpleasant manner.

On several occasions, Mary hears someone weeping in another part of the house. When she asks questions, the servants become evasive. She goes exploring and discovers her uncle's son, Colin, a lonely, bedridden boy as petulant and disagreeable as Mary used to be. His father shuns him because the child closely resembles his mother. Mr. Craven is a mild hunchback, and both he and Colin are morbidly convinced that the boy will develop the same condition. Colin accepts Mary and insists on her visiting him often.

Dickon and Mary take Colin outside in a wheelchair so he can see his mother's garden. He visits it with them whenever the weather allows. As the garden revives and flourishes, so does Colin. He resolves to walk and run like a normal boy by the next time his father returns home; to accomplish these aims, he carries out a program of simple physical exercises and positive thinking. He makes great progress, but they conceal it from the rest of the household with the pretense that he is still an invalid.

Mr. Craven arrives while the children are outdoors and he is drawn toward the secret garden. As he approaches, he is astonished to hear their voices inside the walls; Colin bursts out of the garden door toward him, winning a footrace against Mary and Dickon. They take Mr. Craven into the secret garden to tell him everything.

On Arbour Day, in the morning, we took all of our books out of our desks, and washed the desks with soap and water. In the afternoon the teacher took us on a picnic. I enjoyed playing baseball at school. In winter time Miss Young asked the pupils what they would like for lunch the next day. There was a cook stove in the school, so we brought the food and she cooked it for us. Sometimes it was baked potatoes, various kinds of soup, rice pudding, and other hot treats to supplement our packed lunches. Sure tasted good on a cold day.

I did very well in most subjects, especially memory work (Literature), maps (Geography), dates (British and Canadian History), quite often getting 100 in Arithmetic, Grammar and Spelling. Each year we put on a play for our families and the neighbourhood. Typically it was a Christmas story with Mary and Joseph, baby Jesus (a doll), angels, the shepherds and the wise men.

I got very cold as soon as I went outside in the winter due to the fact that I was so thin. My fingers and toes would soon feel frozen. To help stay warm, I always wore a second pair of gloves or mittens and an extra warm pair of woolen socks. My cousin Rosa, who was a year older than me, gave me a pair of ice skates in Malvern. I enjoyed them immensely. Rosa challenged me to go down a big hill, in a field, that was covered with ice. We made it to the bottom, still standing on our feet, but, oh boy! It was a bumpy ride. We skated on the river or nearby pond.

The nearest High School would have required a five mile walk each morning, then a tram ride, and the same back again every afternoon. Instead, I walked three miles each way, and attended one year of Continuation School in Agincourt in 1934-35. My next door neighbour, Myrna Clements, and I went together and shared a locker. On some days of the week we were fortunate to get a ride with a man who regularly travelled that highway into Toronto. He owned a nice car and we felt he must be rich! There wasn't the fear of harm from strangers that later generations of children had to be warned about.

Myrna's sister took us to a dance in Malvern and I danced the progressive barn dance, as well as other dances. It was fun to get together with other boys and girls our ages in a social setting.

Our courses were English Grammar, Spelling and Speech Writing, French, French Grammar, Latin, Music, Art, Arithmetic, Geography, Agriculture, Chemistry and Physical Education (high jumping, relay races). Dad built me a high jump outfit in our backyard so that I could practice at home. My team came second in a relay race at the Agincourt and Stouffville School Field Day in 1934. Mom and Dad were there to watch me. I successfully completed one speech on, "My Day at the Ploughing Match," but didn't do as well on another one.

Mr. Kennedy was my form teacher, who taught us Agriculture, among other things. He took us outside for walks so that we could identify different plants; we also dug up the ground and planted a garden to watch plants grow. Once we walked a short distance from the school to see Uncle Tom's Cabin. We weren't able to see inside the log cabin that day because it was locked up and no one was there. However, we did walk through rows of lilac trees, all different kinds from different countries of the world. They were beautiful and the smell was fabulous.

Born in Maryland, Josiah Henson worked as a slave for forty-one years. In 1830, he and his family escaped to Upper Canada (Ontario) via the Underground Railroad. Josiah wanted to obtain his own land. In 1841, he moved his family to Dresden and helped to start the Dawn Settlement to provide a refuge and a new beginning for former slaves. Through his leadership, the British American Institute, one of Canada's first industrial schools, was founded for the advancement of fugitive slaves. Josiah Henson's name became synonymous with the central character "Uncle Tom" in Harriet Beecher Stowe's famous novel *Uncle Tom's Cabin*. Stowe, an active abolitionist, wrote the novel in response to the 1850 passage of the second Fugitive Slave Act which punished those who aided runaway slaves and diminished the rights of fugitives as well as freed Blacks. Stowe focused the novel on the character of Uncle Tom, a long-suffering black slave. The novel depicts the reality of slavery while also asserting that Christian love can overcome something as destructive as enslavement of fellow human beings. The novel sold 300,000 copies within the first year and helped to raise awareness to the brutality of slavery. Abraham Lincoln credited the book as being a catalyst of the Civil War.

Chapter 5

There's a piece . . . there's Another One

    The first jigsaw puzzle was produced about 1760 by John Spilsbury, a London engraver and mapmaker. Spilsbury mounted one of his maps on a sheet of hardwood and cut around the borders of the countries using a fine-bladed marquetry saw. The puzzle was used to teach British children their geography. Cardboard puzzles were introduced in the late 1800's for children's puzzles. In the 20th century, cardboard puzzles were die-cut, like a giant cookie-cutter pressed down on the cardboard to make the cut. Puzzles were made more intricate and difficult to appeal to adults as well as to children. It might seem odd at first glance that a non-necessity like a jigsaw puzzle would sell so well in the Depression, but the appeal was that one bought a good deal of entertainment for a small price. Even during difficult times, people continued to buy a puzzle because they found in it an escape from their daily problems and stress. Assembling jigsaw puzzles offered people a sense of accomplishment that they couldn't find anywhere else as the puzzle draws you into its world, giving great satisfaction. The jigsaw puzzle could be worked on by an individual or a group, would occupy one's time enjoyably for hours, and could then be broken up to do again or to pass on to another family member or friend.

    I don't know how old I was when I did my first jigsaw puzzle but I continued working on them throughout my lifetime. I imagine the first one was very simple, maybe a picture of a cat or dog, maybe a picture of Mickey Mouse after I saw the cartoon "Steamboat Willie" in 1929, maybe Popeye the spinach-eating sailor man with his bulging forearms. Cinderella in her gold coach pulled by the mice would have been a beautiful one to complete, or Cinderella in her ball gown dancing with the prince in the brightly lit ballroom filled with colour and laughter. Flowers have always been a love of mine but putting together a jigsaw puzzle of a thousand pieces of a field of flowers can be a real challenge. A mountain scene with a lake is another beauty. Although buildings were never a first choice of subject, I have done many puzzles of them with one of the last ones being a picture of Casa Loma in Toronto. Wild animals of the African grasslands were intriguing to me and a favourite puzzle was a scene of giraffes, zebra, and other animals by the waterhole. For many years I glued my favourite puzzles onto cardboard or thin boards and displayed them around my apartment. I exchanged the pictures as often as I wished.

One of my earliest projects was making scrapbooks of movie stars and of the Dionne Quintuplets. Many years later, I made scrapbooks for my young granddaughters. I found colourful pictures on calendars and in magazines that I thought might interest them—one book had pictures of animals, another book had scenery.

Dad made a swing for Willie and me that he hung in the doorway of the garage in Belleville. Sometimes Willie would give me a push. It was quite something to really get going. On the back swing, it was dark in the garage, but when I moved forward all of a sudden a beautiful, bright, sunny day emerged with the clouds floating in the deep blue sky. But before long it was the roof of the shed that was dimly seen. For long periods of time I could be quite content swinging away. When it was time for Willie to have a turn, I might bounce my ball against the shed, as I performed actions to the rhyme: "1, 2, 3 a-lary; 4, 5, 6 a-lary; 7, 8, 9 a-lary; 10 a-lary postman." I enjoyed hopscotch, skipping single and double dutch, playing with jacks, and a yo-yo. I might put on my roller skates for a trip down the sidewalk. The roller skates had ball bearing wheels, with the skates clipping onto my shoes with a special key to tighten them. Willie and I shared a wagon, in which I would zoom along the street at great speed.

Dad bought us a bat and ball; together with the neighbourhood children, we often played baseball on some empty lots across the road from our house. Another game went like this: "Lemonade in the shade; what's your trade and how do you do it?" Then we acted it out and others guessed what it was.

Nellie Ainsworth sometimes organized games for all the kids. For one game, she would divide the group into two, taking one group and hiding them. In the dirt of their laneway, she drew a map to the hiding place. The other group would have to figure out from the map where they were hidden and go and find them.

I liked paper doll cutouts and played with them a lot. Beginning in the 1830s, celebrity paper dolls featured entertainers such as ballerinas and characters from the P. T. Barnum Circus, as well as British royalty. In 1838 when Charles Fenerty made the first paper newsprint from wood pulp, the price of paper became much cheaper. Paper dolls were affordable for more families. The dolls themselves were printed on cardboard and had to be cut out with scissors. Mom did the cutting out when I was small. As I got a little older I was able to manage the scissors and cut out all of the outfits. The paper dolls and their costumes now come with perforations around them and can be gently punched out of the pages—much easier than in the 1920s and 1930s! The outfits had little tabs to fold down to hold them on the dolls.

I could dress my dolls to go to a fancy ball and imagine that I was the fairy godmother dressing Cinderella in the most gorgeous ball gown and dainty glass slippers. I could dress the handsome prince in a tuxedo and just imagine the love in his eyes when he met and danced with Cinderella.

Do you see the ballroom filled with women dressed in beautiful gowns of all the colours of the rainbow—red and pink, yellow and gold, pale green and grass green, sky blue and royal blue, mauve and deep purple. The jewels sparkled in the lamplight. The men could be quite colourful in their evening dress as well. If the tuxedos were black, navy or slate gray, the cummerbunds shone in lively colours.

Sometimes I would imagine that I was Cinderella—the excitement I felt, the wonder of gathering in the ballroom, something I had never before experienced. Then meeting a handsome man and dancing with him—not even realizing that he was the prince of the land—then my panic just before midnight remembering the instructions to leave by then and fleeing from the ballroom and losing a slipper as I flew down the grand staircase and into the night.

Another day I might dress the dolls to go to a ball game. Going shopping was always fun. Dressing to go to the beach always had me remembering our visits to the lake, our picnic lunches under the shade of a big tree, Dad fishing, while I played in the sand.

Dad was very good at whittling and made many of my toys. A prized possession was the beautiful doll house he built for me with wooden furniture. Mom made the bedding and cushions for the chairs. I was thrilled with it! I would sit by the doll house, talking away to myself. Sometimes I was the Mother, sometimes the little girl. I had a Dad and brother too, just like in real life. Our neighbour had a new little baby so I pretended I had one in my dollhouse family—reading the baby a story, singing the baby to sleep. Dad made a cradle to rock the baby—Mom made sheets and blankets to fit.

Dad built the doll house just like the home we lived in. On the main floor there was a living room, complete with a couch, rocking chair, a rug in the centre of the room, and a fireplace at one end. At the two windows there were curtains that could be opened and closed. Dad made a miniature teacher's desk like the full size version he made for me. There were miniature pictures on the wall—one was of Buckingham Palace in England. No house would be complete without a picture of King George V and Queen Mary. It was during King George's reign that women were allowed to vote for the first time.

The dining room had a large table with six chairs, a china cabinet which held my set of dishes which were perfect for having a tea party. Sometimes Mom would give me a cookie to break up into small pieces so that there was some on each plate for the family sitting around the table for tea. There was a wooden cabinet to hold the table cloth and napkins that Mom made. The drawers pulled out and the doors opened.

In the kitchen there was a metal stove complete with a drop-down oven door. There were pans to place on the stove to cook the supper for the family. Today we will have roast beef, potatoes and fresh peas from the garden. The icebox had a door that opened and a block of "ice" made out of wood to keep the food cool. There was a bottle of milk, a pound of butter, an apple and a banana. There was a sink to wash the dishes after the meal was eaten.

The curved staircase off the kitchen led upstairs to the bedrooms and the bathroom. In my dollhouse, all the rooms upstairs belonged to our family. There was a large bedroom for Mom and Dad with deep burgundy curtains at the windows. Mom made the bedding in just the right colours for each room.

The little girl's room had a beautiful pink cover on the bed. The dresser, complete with a mirror, had a brush and comb set and a little jar of perfume to sit on the dresser scarf. The drawers that opened had little clothes painted inside them—the drawers were just big enough for my little treasures—brightly coloured stones found at the beach, ball and jacks set, pretty marbles. The curtains at the window were white with pink roses. The window opened to look out to the front of the house where there were wide steps up to the veranda. I could look down at the flower boxes under the windows and imagine the beautiful flowers growing there.

In the playroom Dad made toys for the children to play with. He made a beautiful rocking horse, blocks for building, cars and trucks, even a doll or two. A miniature bat and ball were added and sometimes would be found in the boy's room. Mom bought a metal bathtub for the bathroom and Dad whittled a sink and toilet. There were little towels hanging on the towel racks, a mirror hanging above the sink and a holder for miniature toothbrushes.

When I was young, Mom enjoyed reading books to me. The fairy tales of Little Red Riding Hood, Cinderella, Sleeping Beauty and Puss 'n' Boots were popular stories, as was Alice's Adventures in Wonderland by Lewis Carroll. The library was a must stop with my brother and I walking uptown once a week. I loved to read and would devour books. When I was a little older, I would read a book in one night.

Another exciting time was when the circus came to town. I would sit on the front veranda eating my breakfast and watch the colourful wagons go by on their way from the train station to the fairgrounds. A circus is a travelling company of performers including acrobats, clowns, trained animals, trapeze acts, tightrope walkers, and other stunt-oriented artists performing to music. A circus is held in an oval or circular arena with tiered seating around its edge, usually in a large tent called the big top.

One time my brother went to the station at 4:00 a.m. to watch the circus train come in. He got a job looking after Tom Mix's horse.

Tom Mix, an American film actor, and the star of many early Western movies, made over three hundred films between 1910 and 1935, all but nine of which were silent features. He was Hollywood's first Western megastar and helped define the genre for all cowboy actors who followed. He grew up in Dubois, Pennsylvania where he learned to ride horses while working on the local farm owned by John Dubois, a lumber businessman. He had dreams of being in the circus one day. In 1905 Mix rode in Theodore Roosevelt's inaugural parade with a group of 50 horsemen. Mix began his film career as a supporting cast member with the Selig Polyscope Company. His first shoot in 1910 at their studio in the Edendale district of Los Angeles (now known as Echo Park) was *Ranch Life in the Great Southwest*, in which he showed his skills as a cattle wrangler. The film was a success and Mix became an early motion picture star. In 1917 Tom Mix signed with Fox Film Corporation. He made more than 160 cowboy films throughout the 1920s. These featured action oriented scripts which contrasted with the documentary style of his work with Selig. Heroes and villains were sharply defined and a clean-cut cowboy always "saved the day." Millions of North American children grew up watching his films on Saturday afternoons, myself among them. His intelligent and handsome horse Tony also became a celebrity. Mix did his own stunts and was frequently injured.

His performances weren't noted for their realism but for screen-friendly action stunts and horseback riding, attention-grabbing cowboy costumes and showmanship. At the Edendale lot Mix built a 12-acre shooting set called Mixville. Loaded with western props and furnishings, it has been described as a "complete frontier town, with a dusty street, hitching rails, a saloon, jail, bank, doctor's office, surveyor's office, and the simple frame houses typical of the early Western era." Near the back of the lot an Indian village of lodges was ringed by miniature plaster mountains which on screen were very convincing. The set also included a simulated desert, large corral and a ranch house with no roof to facilitate interior shots.

Tom Mix was "the King of Cowboys" when Ronald Reagan and John Wayne were youngsters and the influence of his screen persona can be seen in their approach to portraying cowboys. In 1929 Mix was a pallbearer at the funeral of Wyatt Earp.

Mix's last screen appearance was a 15-episode Mascot Pictures serial, *The Miracle Rider* (1935). That year Texas governor James Allred named Mix an honorary Texas Ranger.

Tom Mix was performing in the circus in our town with his horse. We were given a half day off school to go to the circus. The lions, tigers, elephants and horses were enthralling to watch as they performed for us. Being in the cage with the tigers and lions would have taken a lot of nerve.

Chapter 6

The Great Depression

If God brings you to it, He will bring you through it.

> Happy moments, praise God.
> Difficult moments, seek God.
> Quiet moments, worship God.
> Painful moments, trust God.
> Every moment, thank God.

During the 1920s in Canada, the times were pretty good. Western farm crops were good, and mining, fishing and lumbering flourished. Manufacturing was at a high level and employment was steady.

But there were danger signals. Wheat, Canada's chief export, was being over-produced around the world and the 1928 Canadian crop had not been sold in 1929. The economies of many European countries were shaky and had been since the First World War. Factories, especially in the United States, were over-producing, and since the market couldn't take the goods, their inventories and stockpiles were soon huge. The values of stocks on the New York Stock Exchange were grossly overvalued, but government and business appeared to ignore the signs. Things would get better and bigger, they predicted.

Canada was in a very vulnerable position. Despite the country's vast size, her thinly-spread population numbered only about 10,000,000. Her revenues came from export sales, and these sales were in vulnerable commodities—grain, pulp and paper, metals. The U.S. accounted for forty per cent of our export sales, and Canada counted on the Americans for vital money for expansion.

In October 1929, all the black clouds met in one place, the New York Stock Exchange, and the thunderbolt struck. Stock prices fell disastrously, a sign that the American Economic System had crashed. Canada's markets began to collapse. The U.S., to protect its own, erected high tariff walls, shutting out Canadian goods. The prairie wheat economy tottered as the $1.60 a bushel price of 1929 skidded to 38 cents. Even the weather had turned against us with a drought destroying the West.

The Great Depression was a worldwide economic downturn having devastating effects in every country, rich or poor. International trade plunged by half to two-thirds, as did personal income, tax revenue, prices and profits. Cities all around the world were hit hard, especially those dependent on heavy industry. Construction was halted in many countries. Farming and rural areas suffered as crop prices fell by roughly 60 percent. Facing plummeting demand with few alternate sources of jobs, areas dependent on farming, mining and logging suffered the most.

Farmers stopped buying. Eastern factories closed, or laid off hundreds. Construction stopped. Banks no longer lent money; instead, they called in loans. Less money was put into circulation, fewer goods were produced, more factories were shut down, the rolls of the poor grew longer, and gloom and despair deepened.

The decline in the US economy was the factor that pulled down most other countries at first, then internal weaknesses or strengths in each country made conditions worse or better.

When the upturn began in Canada around 1937 or 1938, it was a long, long struggle. The rains came to the prairies and that helped, and more and more men went back to work, but wages were still miserably low. Hundreds of thousands were still on direct public relief—a massive drain on the purse of a country that had precious little revenue anyway. Special projects and programs were reviving parts of the economy and the future did look brighter, but nobody could say that they really saw the end of it all.

In Europe, Hitler's troops were marching into Austria and then into Czechoslovakia, and wise men knew that it was only a matter of time before Germany would smash into Poland. On September 1, 1939, Hitler gave the order and his tanks rolled. The Second World War had begun. On September 10, Canada declared war and a vast military effort got under way which was to require the services of every available man and woman for the next six years, in the armed forces, in defense plants, in factories and on farms across the nation. Everyone was at work.

The Great Depression was over. It had not been solved by the best brains in the country juggling with economic theories, but by the demands of total war, courtesy of Adolf Hitler.

During the early 1930's, the clothes I wore were mostly somebody else's hand-me-downs. In 1932 we moved to Malvern. One summer while there, our well went dry and we got water from a neighbour. We had to fill a washtub, and carry it on our wagon, pulling it along the gravel road. We lost some as the water splashed out on the bumpy journey home. At corners of the house large wooden barrels were placed to catch rain water which was nice and soft for washing our hair. We didn't have a bathroom or running water in the house, only a sink to take dirty water away. We took baths in the washtub in the kitchen.

While living in Malvern, I was invited to spend a week or two of my summer holidays with Alice Allen, who lived on Waverley Avenue in Toronto. We would go to the show quite often, if we could get someone to buy children's tickets for us. It was too expensive to pay full price. These were the years of the Depression, during the early 1930's. Once when our family stayed overnight at Allens', we were awakened by a heavy earth tremor. I remember my bed shaking.

We had visited Dad's brother, Jack, and his family once when we were in Toronto attending the CNE, before my Aunt died (December 8, 1931). Jack and Elizabeth Todd had eight children with the oldest two daughters being married. Ivy married Albert Worne and had a young daughter and a newborn son by this time. They lived near us for awhile before moving to Toronto. Violet (*Dids*) was married to Howard Stanley Feeney and they had three children, Iris, Patricia and John. The other children, John, Robert Samuel, Bessie, Albert (*Tarz*), Rosa and Ernie were still at home. Rosa was a year older than me and we spent many hours together. Ernie was a year younger. Bessie married Bob Bond on July 1, 1934 and moved to Toronto.

We spent many Sunday evenings at Uncle Jack Todd's or at his daughter, Violet "Dids" Feeney's home. The Todds were a musical family, John played the accordion, Bob made the violin sing, Tarz played guitar and Jew's harp, Rosa taught herself to play the piano, and Ernie had a lovely singing voice to harmonize with his sisters and brothers. Their friends would join us and we danced to the music.

The singing of the birds, the soothing sound of rustling leaves, the clear sky full of sparkling stars at night, beautiful sunrises and sunsets that can be seen more easily in the open countryside are some of the benefits of country living. We had a large yard and planted a big vegetable garden, big enough to sell some of the vegetables to others. Dad and Uncle Jack tried their hand at market gardening, also at growing mushrooms. Dad did some shoe repairing as he owned a stitching machine to stitch the soles to the uppers. Willie got work, here and there, on farms around the area; he joined the York Rangers. One summer, Rosa, Mom and I went berry picking to earn some money, picking strawberries, raspberries, black and red currants and gooseberries. Times were tough and everyone did everything they could to survive.

There were downsides to being out in the country in the 1930s. We had no running water in the house, but instead had a well outside. The pump had to be primed before pumping to fill the pails to bring inside. On wash day, a lot of water had to be pumped and then heated on the stove—an all day event. We did not have an indoor flush toilet, but instead had an outhouse. This wasn't too bad from spring to fall, except for the spiders and other bugs that liked to make their homes inside, but it sure was cold in the winter, inconvenient when it was raining and very dark at night. Flashlights were not common then, the first one invented in 1902. Our source of light was kerosene lanterns.

I missed the friends I had grown up with in Belleville but there were new friends to make from my new school and the neighbours, including our Todd relatives with their growing families.

After being without a regular job for about four years, Dad decided to go back to England. Things were opening up faster there after the Depression. He left in the spring of 1935 and soon got work as a labourer for the County Council in Grays, Essex, working on the roads. Mom, Willie and I stayed behind until we heard good news from Dad.

Chapter 7

The Long Ride

Mom arranged for an auction sale for all the household effects. Our house was not sold until after we were living in England. I remember Mom sitting on the stairs, all upset, while the sale went on. Everything was sold except our clothes and bedding and perhaps a few mementos. It was sad for me to see my dolls' house, books and teacher's desk go. Dad had made the desk especially for me because I played school a lot, many times by myself. I would be the teacher, asking the questions, and the pupils answering, as well.

Dad asked us to bring the kitchen cabinet, a sack of apples from our tree, and the big clock that hung on the wall. The cabinet was put in two crates and filled with our bedding and pillows. It went into the ship's hold with other luggage, but Willie had the responsibility of looking after the apples, and the fragile clock, carrying them whenever necessary, all the way to their destination.

After the auction sale, a milkman gave us a ride into Toronto in his milk truck. We stayed overnight at cousin Ivy Worne's house. I usually got sick whenever travelling by bus, car or train. Someone suggested sucking lemons on the train trip from Toronto to Montreal, which I did, and I was fine.

Then on November 8, 1935, we boarded the Ship R.M.S. Alaunia of the Cunard Lines and sailed to England.

The *Alaunia* is from the great age of Atlantic sea passenger travel, a time when the Royal Mail Steam Packet Company, the Cunard Line represented the finest and most luxurious way of crossing the Atlantic. The company's slogan summed up the prevailing view at the time—'Getting there is half the fun'. Founded in 1839 by a resident of Nova Scotia, Mr Samuel Cunard, the Cunard Line grew from humble beginnings. Realizing the early successes of steam ships crossing the Atlantic, Samuel took a brave gamble and risked his entire fortune along with 31 other shareholders to build the first of the Cunard Steamship Company Limited's fleet, the 200-feet long, 32-feet in the beam, two wooden paddle steamship, *Britannia*, which was built on the Clyde.

The *Britannia* was launched on February 7, 1840 and set off on its maiden crossing of the Atlantic on July 4, 1840 with Samuel Cunard aboard for the voyage which took twelve days and fifteen hours. The construction and acquisition of more ships followed. Although the early ships were constructed from wood, from 1853 onwards all Cunard ships were built of iron and later steel. The new construction promised greater strength and flexibility in shipbuilding and led to the development of the more efficient screw propulsion.

By 1907, the passenger trade had evolved from the spartan *Britannia*, which Charles Dickens had called on its maiden voyage a 'hearse with windows', to large, spacious vessels that provided great luxuries at sea. In this year Cunard reached new heights of excellence with the construction of the *Lusitania* and the *Mauretania*. These vast floating palaces were inspired by architectural and decorative styles found on land and mimicked the look of the great London hotels.

The *Alaunia* I was built in 1913 in the run-up to the First World War, the second of three ships launched on June 9, 1913. She weighed 13,405 tons gross and had twin-screw quadruple-expansion engines, which developed 8,500hp, enough to push her and her sister ships *Andania* and *Aurania* to a top speed of 14.5 knots. The *Alaunia* was constructed of steel with three decks and bridge superstructure, which gave her a total height of 243 feet. She was 540 feet long with a beam of 64 feet. On board was accommodation for 520 second class and 1,620 third-class passengers. The usual third-class dormitories were replaced in this vessel by four- and six-berth cabins. She carried a crew of 289.

The *Alaunia, Andania* and *Aurania* were identical vessels, each fitted with two masts and two towering funnels amidships in the Cunard Line's classic red with black bands at the top.

The *Alaunia* made its maiden voyage on November 27, 1913 from Liverpool to Boston via Queenstown and Portland, arriving in Boston on December 6. She made regular Atlantic crossings throughout the first half of

1914 taking emigrants to new lives in America. In August 1914 the Alaunia was requisitioned as a troopship, with the *Andania* being requisitioned two months later. The ships carried troops to Europe from Canada and America. It was in this role that the *Alaunia* left London on September 19, 1916 on a return voyage to New York. On October 19, having safely crossed the dangerous Atlantic, as she headed up the English Channel for London, she was suddenly rocked by an enormous explosion—she had struck a mine. The damage caused by the mine explosion was too severe and the order was given to abandon the ship. All passengers and 163 of the crew were safely taken ashore, with two of the crew losing their lives. The *Alaunia's* sister ship, *Andania,* also failed to survive the war as she was torpedoed and sunk by a German U-boat to the north of Rathlin Island lighthouse with the loss of seven people.

On February 7, 1925, S.S. Alaunia II was launched. It was the last of the six 14,000 ton "A-class" liners built for Cunard in the early 1920's. There was accommodation for 500 cabin passengers, and 1,200 third class passengers. Its maiden voyage on July 24 was from Liverpool to Quebec and Montreal. In 1939 the ship was requisitioned for service as an armed merchant cruiser for use in the Second World War.

Mom and I shared a cabin together. The first night sleeping on the top bunk bothered me being so close to the ceiling. After that night, the steward made up my bed opposite Mom's bed, on the daytime couch. The cabins were very small, you could hardly turn around in them.

On the ship we met the Carrier Family. Anne was about my age and we chummed around together on the trip. As a teenager in Malvern I listened to the radio a lot. I had paper and a pencil nearby at all times and whenever the latest songs were sung I copied down the words. Anne and I spent a lot of the time singing these hit songs. Mr. Carrier had hurt his back so when they embarked he was immediately placed in sick bay; he died on board ship and was buried at sea. That was quite an experience for me, a fifteen year old! The coffin was draped in a flag and, after the funeral service on the deck of the ship, the coffin slid down a ramp into the sea.

Mom got sick going across the ocean and had to stay in bed for a time. Surprisingly, I was fine until we entered the English Channel. That was more than my stomach could stand!

From the deck we saw Dad waiting for us at the dock. The first thing we noticed when we disembarked was that Dad didn't have a moustache—all my life I had known him with one!

Chapter 8

Bridges, Bridges Everywhere

After travelling to Grays Essex, about 20 miles from London, we went shopping for furniture. It was raining and foggy which didn't help our feelings any as we were none too excited to have left Canada.

We lived first in a council house (several houses attached to one another) at 55 William Street. There was no electricity upstairs; we had to buy kerosene lamps to use in the bedrooms. There was no indoor bathroom; we took a bath in a metal washtub in the pantry. There was a flush toilet in a small shed attached to the house, outside the back door, almost like an outhouse but not quite the same.

Soon after our arrival, Dad took us to London to show us all the sights (Tower of London, Westminster Abbey, St. Paul's Cathedral, British Museum, Marble Arch, Big Ben by the Parliament Buildings, Buckingham Palace), some of which I had learned about at school. Packed into the 610 square miles of Greater London are a wealth of concert halls, art galleries, museums, parks and gardens, theatres, cinemas, restaurants and famous buildings. With its "bobbies", its red double-decker buses and its famous underground system, London has an unhurried air of permanence reinforced by the durability of its great institutions. Seeing these sites was awe inspiring. At the age of sixteen, everything seemed bigger than I had ever imagined. And London was so big, stretching on for miles. Descriptions of the sites and an occasional black and white picture did not do justice to the wonder of the actual sites—it was like the difference between a picture of an ice cream cone compared to a maple walnut ice cream cone in my hand held close to my mouth for my tongue to lick its sweet, cold refreshment.

London evolved as two separate towns—the walled fortress founded by the Romans about AD 43 and the settlement around Westminster Abbey some 900 years later, the two separated by only a mile or two of marshy ground. The Roman town developed after they forded the Thames between the gravel banks of Ludgate Hill on the north bank and Southwark on the south, to allow their troops and transport landing on the Kentish coast, access to their chief city, Colchester, to the north east and their other outposts to the north and west. Within a few years this crossing point became the hub of Roman activities in Britain.

Under Emperor Constantius, whose wife was a Briton, London flourished and at the beginning of the 3rd century AD its citizens enjoyed a standard of living that was not attained again until nearly 1500 years later. The Roman presence in Britain was short lived, and the country under the Angles, Saxons and Jutes reverted to a farming economy with London being largely abandoned. The Norman William rebuilt London's fortifications, added the White Tower castle, and had another church built on the St. Paul's site. Ludgate Hill, the highest point of the City of London, is crowned by the Anglican St. Paul's Cathedral, being the seat of the Bishop of London, and is a major tourist attraction. It has had several major reconstructions since medieval times, with the current construction designed by Christopher Wren, built of Portland stone, with a dome rising 365 feet to the cross at its summit, the dome being inspired by St. Peter's Basilica in Rome. Wren achieved a pleasing appearance by building three domes: the tall outer dome is non-structural but impressive to view; the lower inner dome provides an artistically balanced interior, and between the two is a structural cone that supports the apex structure and the outer dome. The cathedral was completed on October 20, 1708, Wren's 76th birthday.

With the arrival of Henry VIII on the throne, Westminster's destiny was uprooted. He moved the court out of Westminster Palace in favour of the Palace of Whitehall, formerly the London residence of the Archbishops of York, and with the dissolution of the monasteries Westminster Abbey became a Protestant Church and St. Stephen's Hall the home of the Commons. By the time Elizabeth I was on the throne, the combined population of London and Westminster was around 130,000, living in cramped, dirty accommodation with sewage running down the streets from the overflowing Fleet river. The

Civil War of the Roundheads and the Cavaliers brought about the unification of London and Westminster into the largest city in Europe. Twenty years later the old London disappeared, first in the Plague, which accounted for more than 50,000 lives, then the great fire in 1666 which burned for four days, demolished 13,000 dwellings and left 70,000 homeless, many of them camping in the open outside the city walls.

The city fathers had an opportunity to redesign London. Sir Christopher Wren drew up plans for a column containing a cantilevered stone staircase of 311 steps leading to a viewing platform to commemorate the Great Fire and to celebrate the rebuilding of the city. This column was surmounted by a drum and a copper urn from which flames emerged. The Monument is 202 feet high—the distance between it and the site in Pudding Lane where the fire began at the bakery of Thomas Fariner. The Monument provides visitors with an opportunity to look across London in all directions from a height of about 160 feet, the level of the public gallery.

London, the capital city of both England and the United Kingdom, is the largest metropolitan area in the European Union. Throughout its 2,000 year history London has been part of many movements, including the English Renaissance, the Industrial Revolution and the Gothic Revival. The city's core, the ancient City of London, still retains its limited medieval boundaries; but since the 19th century, the name "London" has also referred to the whole metropolis that has developed around it, having a population of about seven and a half million. London is one of the world's most important business, financial and cultural centres and its influence in politics, education, entertainment, media, fashion and the arts contributes to its status as a major global city. It is a major tourist attraction for both domestic and overseas visitors, with annual expenditure by tourists of around £15 billion. It was the host city for the 1908 and 1948 Summer Olympic Games and will host the 2012 Summer Games. Greater London contains four World Heritage sites: the Tower of London, the historic settlement of Greenwich, the Royal Botanical Gardens at Kew, and the site comprising the Palace of Westminster, Westminster Abbey and St. Margaret's Church.

The 16th and 17th centuries saw the City of London grow with the expansion of world trade. The wharves of the Pool of London were thick with sea-going vessels while naval dockyards were built at Deptford. By the 18th century, the Thames was one of the world's busiest waterways, as London became the centre of the vast, mercantile British Empire. London's population draws from a wide range of peoples, cultures, and religions, with over 300 languages being spoken within the city.

The River Thames is a mighty river flowing for 346 kilometres, rising at Thames Head in Gloucestershire a mile north of the village of Kemble and flowing into the North Sea. It is a tidal river having a rise and fall of seven metres in London, having stretches of both seawater and freshwater supporting a variety of wildlife such as the cormorant, gulls, geese, swans, mallard, mandarin and wood ducks, heron and kingfisher. There have been bridges across the River Thames since Roman times, with the first one being built in 43 A.D., each having their different characters and fascinating histories, each offering terrific views, whether passing over them on foot, under them on a river cruise, or looking at them as you stroll along the banks of the river. Having 214 bridges, more than twenty tunnels and one natural ford which is shallow enough to wade across, the river's long tradition of farming, fishing, milling and trade with other nations started with the Saxons and the Romans. King William had many castles built, including those at Wallingford, Rochester, Windsor and the Tower of London. During the reign of King John the multi-piered London Bridge was completed with John licensing the building of houses on the bridge as a direct means of deriving revenue for its maintenance, and it was soon colonized by shops. The medieval bridge had nineteen small arches and a drawbridge with a defensive gatehouse at the southern end.

Until sufficient crossings were established, the river provided a formidable barrier, with Belgic tribes and Anglo-Saxon kingdoms being defined by which side of the river they were on. When English counties were established their boundaries were partly determined by the Thames. On the Northern bank were the traditional counties of Gloucestershire, Oxfordshire, Buckinghamshire, Middlesex and Essex. On the southern bank were the counties of Wiltshire, Berkshire, Surrey and Kent. The bridges and tunnels that have been built have changed the dynamics and made cross-river development and shared responsibilities more practical.

Many of the present road bridges on the river are on the site of earlier fords, ferries and wooden structures. The earliest known major crossings of the Thames by the Romans were at London Bridge and Staines Bridge. Kingston's growth is believed to stem from its having the only crossing between London Bridge and Staines until the beginning of the 18th century when many stone and brick road bridges were built in new locations or to replace existing structures both in London and along the length of the river.

The world's first underwater tunnel was the Thames Tunnel built in 1843 and used to carry the East London Line. The Tower Subway was the first railway under the Thames, which was followed by all the deep-level tube lines. Road tunnels built in East London at the end of the 19th century were the Blackwall Tunnel, the Rotherhithe Tunnel, and the Dartford Crossing Tunnel.

The Woolwich Ferry carries cars and passengers across the river in the Thames Gateway. Upstream are smaller pedestrian ferries, for example Hampton Ferry and Shepperton to Weybridge Ferry, the last being the only non-permanent crossing that remains on the Thames Path.

The river is navigable for large ocean-going ships as far as the Pool of London and London Bridge. The building of a new London Bridge in 1825 with fewer pillars than the old one, allowed the river to flow more freely and reduced the likelihood of freezing over in the winter. During World War II, the protection of the Thames was crucial to the defense of the country.

Tower Bridge is a combined suspension and bascule bridge (a moveable bridge with a counterweight that continuously balances the span, or "leaf," throughout the entire upward swing in providing clearance for boat traffic) over the River Thames. It is close to the Tower of London, which gives it its name. With its twin towers, it is one of the most widely recognized symbols of London.

The bridge consists of two towers which are tied together at the upper level by means of two horizontal walkways which are designed to withstand the horizontal forces exerted by the suspended sections of the bridge to the left and the right. It was very impressive to look at with its chocolate brown paint and a thrill to walk across it. 40,000 cars and trucks use the bridge daily.

Her Majesty's Royal Palace and Fortress, more commonly known as the Tower of London, is a historic monument in central London, on the north bank of the River Thames. The tower is a complex of several buildings set within two concentric rings of defensive walls and a moat.

The tower's primary function was a fortress, a royal palace, and a prison (particularly for high status and royal prisoners, such as the Princes in the Tower and the future Queen Elizabeth I). This last use has led to the phrase "sent to the Tower" (meaning "imprisoned"). It has also served as a place of execution and torture, an armoury, a treasury, a zoo, the Royal Mint, a public records office, an observatory, and since 1303, the home of the Crown Jewels of the United Kingdom.

The site of the first Roman London Bridge was about 20 yards east of the current one, roughly lined up with Fish Street Hill, which took people up to the Roman forum, or marketplace. The first stone bridge to cross the Thames on this spot was finished in 1209, having taken 33 years to build and lasted about 600 years. It had 19 arches, and was a busy thoroughfare, packed with shops and houses, some of them seven storeys high. The River Thames froze and fairs were held on the thick ice. In 1722 when London Bridge was so busy that it became hard to collect the tolls that had to be paid to cross over the bridge, a new rule was introduced. People had to pass on the left, a rule which was then adopted throughout the country.

The nursery rhyme, "London Bridges Falling Down" is said to relate to the many difficulties experienced in bridging the River Thames: London's earlier bridges did indeed "wash away" before a bridge built of "stone so strong" was constructed. It has been suggested that the "fair lady" who is "locked up" is a reference to Queen Eleanor of Aquitaine, one of the most fascinating personalities of Medieval Europe.

In her youth Eleanor was remarkably beautiful, and in her later years she showed evidences of a noble disposition. She is one of the few women of antiquity who have atoned for an ill-spent youth by a wise and benevolent old age. Eleanor of Aquitaine ranks among the greatest of female rulers.

Born around 1122, Eleanor was the daughter of William X, duke of Aquitaine and count of Poitiers. Upon her father's death in 1137, Eleanor inherited Aquitaine and Poitiers. That same year, at the age of 15, she married Louis VII, King of France, bringing to the union her vast possessions from the River Loire to the Pyrenees.

Eleanor was an intelligent woman and was courageous and passionate. Eleanor and her retinue, dressed in battle attire, joined Louis VII on the Second Crusade. On their journey to the Holy Land, they first stopped at Antioch, where Eleanor's uncle, Raymond of Tripoli, had been appointed prince of the city. She renewed her friendship with her kin, spending so much time with him that Louis grew jealous. When Louis prepared to leave for Jerusalem, Eleanor refused to go with him, threatening a divorce. Louis, however, took her by force. The expedition failed and both returned to France in separate ships. While the marriage continued for a time, the couple finally separated after the birth of their second daughter. The marriage was annulled in 1152 and Eleanor's vast estates reverted to her control.

Six weeks after her divorce, Eleanor married Henry, duke of Normandy, who soon afterwards became Henry II of England. During her marriage to

Henry, Eleanor continued to rule Aquitaine, which consisted of Guienne and Gascony. The couple had eight children including Richard Coeur de Lion (Richard the Lionhearted), who ruled England from 1189-1199 and John Lackland who ruled from 1199-1216.

Eleanor was very jealous of her second husband, Henry II. In 1173, she incited her sons to rebel against their father, giving them military support. The revolt failed and Eleanor was thrown into prison, where she remained for sixteen years, until her husband's death. In 1189 she was released from prison by order of her son, Richard, when he took the throne. Richard then proceeded to place her at the head of the government.

While she undoubtedly underwent much deprivation during her imprisonment, she did not, when she obtained power, use it to punish her enemies, but rather devoted herself to deeds of mercy and piety, going from city to city, setting free all persons confined for violating the game laws, which in the latter part of Henry's life, were cruelly enforced. In 1202, Eleanor retired to the monastery at Fontevrault, Anjou, where she died in 1204.

At the northern end of Blackfriars Bridge stands a statue to Queen Victoria, who opened the second bridge here in 1869, a hundred years after the first fixed bridge was built here. The name Blackfriars comes from a monastery that was located nearby. When she opened the bridge, the Queen was booed and hissed by local people whose houses had been demolished to make access to the bridge easier. One hundred years later the bridge was replaced by the present construction.

From Westminster Bridge you can look back and see the magnificent Houses of Parliament. Climbing above them is the tower that holds Big Ben, the bell whose ring is known throughout the world. The bell was made in Whitechapel and brought to Parliament on the river.

The location of the Hampton Court Bridge had been a ferry crossing point since the Tudor period. The first bridge was built by James Clarke from 1752-53, after a 1750 parliamentary bill enabled the construction of a privately owned bridge. It had seven wooden arches. It was replaced by a more sturdy wooden bridge in 1778. In 1864-66, a new bridge was built, consisting of wrought iron lattice girders resting on four cast iron columns. The approach was between battlemented brick walls. The modern bridge is the fourth to be located on the site and was planned to reflect the style of portions of Hampton Court Palace designed by Sir Christopher Wren. The bridge has three arches, and is designed to carry road traffic.

Hampton Court Palace is a royal palace in south west London, though not lived in by the British royal family since the 18th century. The palace is located twelve miles south west of Charing Cross and upstream from Central London. It was originally built for Cardinal Wolsey, a favourite of King Henry VIII, circa 1514; in 1529, when Wolsey fell from favour, the palace was passed to the King, who enlarged it.

The following century, William III's massive rebuilding and expansion project intended to rival Versailles was begun. Work halted in 1694, leaving the palace in two distinct contrasting architectural styles, domestic Tudor and Baroque. While the palace's styles are an accident of fate, a unity exists due to the use of pink bricks and a symmetrical balancing of successive low wings. Today, the palace is open to the public, and is a major tourist attraction.

Westminster Abbey and the Palace of Westminster, also known as the Houses of Parliament, is a complex of buildings built on Thorney Island. It is the seat of the two houses of the Parliament of the United Kingdom (the House of Lords and the House of Commons). The palace lies on the north bank of the River Thames in the London borough of the City of Westminster, close to the government buildings of Whitehall. The palace contains 1,100 rooms, 100 staircases and three miles of corridors. Although the building mainly dates from the 19th century, remaining elements of the original historic buildings include Westminster Hall, used today for major public ceremonial events such as lyings in state, and the Jewel Tower. After a fire in 1834, the present Houses of Parliament were built over the next thirty years. The design incorporated Westminster Hall and the remains of St. Stephen's chapel.

Windsor Castle is the largest inhabited castle in the world and, dating back to the time of William the Conqueror, is the oldest in continuous occupation. The castle's floor area is approximately 484,000 square feet. Together with Buckingham Palace in London and Holyrood Palace in Edinburgh, it is one of the principal official residences of the British monarch. Queen Elizabeth II spends many weekends of the year at the castle, using it for both state and private entertaining. Her other two residences, Sandringham House and Balmoral Castle, are the Royal Family's private homes.

Buckingham Palace, located in the City of Westminster, is a major tourist attraction. It has been a rallying point for the British people at times of national rejoicing and crisis. Originally known as Buckingham House, the building which forms the core of today's palace was a large townhouse built for the Duke of Buckingham in 1703 and acquired by George III in 1761 as a private residence, known as "The Queen's House". It was enlarged over the next 75 years, with three wings around a central courtyard. Buckingham Palace became the official royal palace and London residence of the British monarch on the accession of Queen Victoria in 1837. The last major structural additions were made in the late 19th and early 20th centuries, including the present-day public face of Buckingham Palace. The palace chapel was destroyed by a German bomb in World War II. Buckingham Palace has 775 rooms, including 19 state rooms, 52 royal and guest rooms, 188 staff bedrooms, 92 offices, and 78 bathrooms—that would take quite a cleaning staff. The building is 108 metres long across the front, 120 metres deep (including the central quadrangle) and 24 metres high.

The state rooms form the nucleus of the working Palace and are used regularly by Queen Elizabeth II and members of the royal family for official and state entertaining. Buckingham Palace is one of the world's most familiar buildings and more than 50,000 people visit the palace each year as guests to banquets, lunches, dinners, receptions and the royal garden parties.

Who could visit Buckingham Palace without remaining to see the colourful spectacle of the changing of the guard?

The Queen's Guard is the name given to the contingent of infantry responsible for guarding Buckingham Palace and St. James' Palace in London. Because the Sovereign's official residence is St. James', the guard commander, called the Captain of the Guard, is based there, as are the regiment's colours. The Queen's Guard provides sentries during the day and night and patrols the grounds of the Palace.

The Colour is a large flag, a symbol of honour and has the various campaigns associated with the regiment's history emblazoned upon it. The Regimental Colour is of a single colour, the colour of the uniform collar, lapels and cuffs of the regiment, with the insignia of the regiment in the centre. Woven onto the colours are battle honours; the Queen's Colour has honours from the First World War and Second World War, while the Regimental Colour has honours from other campaigns, such as the Sphinx emblem carried by regiments who took part in the Egypt campaign of 1801.

The ceremony of Changing of the Guards takes place in the forecourt of Buckingham Palace about 11 a.m. The St. James' Palace detachment of the queen's Guard is led by the Corps of Drums, bearing the flag. If the Queen is in residence, then the flag will be the Queen's Colour; if she is not in residence, it is the Regimental Colour. They march along the

Mall to Buckingham Palace, where the Buckingham Palace detachment has formed to await their arrival. These two detachments are the Old Guard. Meanwhile the New Guard is forming up, and is inspected by the Adjutant on the parade square at Wellington Barracks while the Band of at least thirty-five musicians plays music. Then the Band leads the New Guard as they march across into the forecourt of Buckingham Palace. The Old Guard presents arms, followed by the New Guard presenting arms. The Captains of the Guards march towards each other for the handing over of the Palace keys. The new reliefs are marched to the guardrooms of Buckingham Palace and St. James' Palace where new sentries are posted. During this time the Band continues to play to entertain the Guards and the watching crowds. The two regimental colours are paraded up and down by the ensigns.

The Buckingham Palace Garden is the largest private garden in London. The Garden is situated at the rear of the palace and occupies a forty-two acre site and has two-and-a-half miles of gravel paths. The planting is varied and exotic, with a mulberry tree dating back to the time of James I of England. In the Garden there is a summerhouse, a helicopter pad, and a tennis court. The artificial lake was completed in 1828 and is supplied with water from the Serpentine, a river which runs through Hyde Park, a river graced by a flock of flamingoes and the Waterloo Vase.

The Waterloo Vase is a great urn, fifteen feet high and weighing twenty tons, fashioned from a single piece of Carrara marble. The Emperor Napoleon I of France when passing through Tuscany on his journey to the Russian front was shown a single massive block of marble which he asked to be preserved for him. It is thought that Napoleon may have ordered it to be roughly hewn into the present urn shape, leaving the panels undecorated in readiness to commemorate his anticipated victories.

Following the French defeat in the Napoleonic Wars, the vase was presented unfinished to the Prince Regent in 1815 by Ferdinand, Grand Duke of Tuscany. The Prince Regent, soon to become George IV, had the vase completed by the sculptor Richard Westmacott with the intention that it be the focal point of the new Waterloo chamber at Windsor Castle, commemorating the Battle of Waterloo. The vase was carved with bas-reliefs of George III on his throne, Napoleon unhorsed, and various allegorical figures. Two winged busts of angels leap incongruously from the sides of the vase, resembling more the figureheads of an ancient ship than the handles of an elegant marble vase.

No floor could bear the weight of the vase, so Edward VII had the vase placed outside in the garden at Buckingham Palace.

Elizabeth II (Elizabeth Alexandra Mary; born April 21, 1926) is the reigning queen of sixteen independent states known as the Commonwealth realms: the United Kingdom of Great Britain and Northern Ireland, Canada, Australia, New Zealand, Jamaica, Barbados, the Bahamas, Grenada, Papua New Guinea, the Solomon Islands, Tuvalu, Saint Lucia, Saint Vincent and the Grenadines, Belize, Antigua and Barbuda, and Saint Kitts and Nevis. Altogether, these countries have a combined population of over 129 million. She holds each crown separately and equally in a shared monarchy, and carries out duties in and on behalf of all the states of which she is sovereign. She is also Head of the Commonwealth, Supreme Governor of the Church of England, Duke of Normandy, Lord of Mann, and Paramount Chief of Fiji.

Her long reign of 58 years has seen sweeping changes, including the dissolution of the British Empire and the evolution of the Commonwealth of Nations. Elizabeth became Queen of the United Kingdom, Canada, Australia, New Zealand, South Africa, Pakistan and Ceylon (now Sri Lanka) upon the death of her father, George VI, on February 6, 1952. As other British colonies gained independence from the United Kingdom, she became queen of several newly independent countries.

Elizabeth married Prince Philip on November 20, 1947. Before the marriage, Philip renounced his Greek and Danish titles, and adopted the style *Lieutenant Philip Mountbatten*, the surname adopted by his mother's family. Just before the wedding, he was created Duke of Edinburgh and granted the style of *His Royal Highness*.

The Commonwealth had not yet completely rebounded from the devastation of the war; rationing still required that the Princess save up her rationing coupons to buy the material for her wedding gown, designed by Norman Hartnell.

Norman Hartnell, an English fashion designer appointed dressmaker to the British Royal Family in 1938, designed the dresses worn by Queen Elizabeth II on her marriage to Prince Philip and for her coronation. The dress designed for the Queen's wedding contained 10,000 seed pearls and many thousands of white crystal beads. Hartnell also designed dresses for Elizabeth, The Queen Mother and Queen Mary.

The wedding was seen as the first glimmer of a hope of rebirth. Elizabeth and Philip received over 2,500 wedding gifts from around the world. At the ceremony, Elizabeth's bridesmaids were her sister Margaret; her cousin,

Princess Alexandra of Kent; Lady Caroline Montagu-Douglas-Scott, a cadet relative through their mutual aunt; Princess Alice, Duchess of Gloucester; her second cousin, Lady Mary Cambridge; Lady Elizabeth Mary Lambart (now Longman), daughter of Frederick Lambart, Earl of Cavan; The Honourable Pamela Mountbatten (now Hicks), Philip's cousin; and two maternal cousins, The Honourable Margaret Elphinstone (now Rhodes) and The Honourable Diana Bowes-Lyon (now Somervell). Her page boys were her young paternal first cousins, Prince William of Gloucester and Prince Michael of Kent. In post-war Britain, it was not acceptable for any of the Duke of Edinburgh's German relations to be invited to the wedding, including Philip's three surviving sisters.

Elizabeth gave birth to her first child, Prince Charles, on November 14, 1948, several weeks after letters patent were issued by her father allowing her children to enjoy a royal and princely status to which they otherwise would not have been entitled. A second child, Princess Anne was born in 1950.

In early 1952, Elizabeth and Philip set out for a tour of Australia and New Zealand via Kenya. At Sagana Lodge, 100 miles north of Nairobi, word arrived of the death of Elizabeth's father on February 6. Philip broke the news to the new queen. The royal party hastily returned to the United Kingdom, and the new Queen and Duke of Edinburgh moved into Buckingham Palace.

The Queen's coronation was held in Westminster Abbey on June 2, 1953, with the ceremony being televised throughout the Commonwealth, and watched by an estimated twenty million people, with twelve million more listening on the radio. Elizabeth wore a gown consisting of embroidered floral emblems of the countries of the Commonwealth: the Tudor rose of England, the Scots thistle, the Welsh leek, shamrocks for Ireland, the wattle of Australia, the maple leaf of Canada, the New Zealand fern, South Africa's protea, two lotus flowers for India and Ceylon, and Pakistan's wheat, cotton and jute.

The Tudor rose is the traditional floral heraldic emblem of England and takes its name and origins from the Tudor dynasty. The thistle is an ancient Celtic symbol of nobility of character as well as of birth, for the wounding or provocation of a thistle yields punishment. The leek is one of the national emblems of Wales. According to one legend, King Cadwaladr of Gwynedd ordered his soldiers to identify themselves by wearing the vegetable on their helmets in an ancient battle against the Saxons that took place in a leek field. The shamrock is a symbol of Ireland, with its three-leafed old white clover. The bark of various Australian species, known as wattles, is very rich in tannin and is an important article of export. The maple leaf is the national symbol of Canada. The Silver Fern is widely used in New Zealand. Together with the Springbok Antelope, the Protea, a flowering plant sometimes called a sugarbush, were treated as a national symbol in South Africa. From ancient times the lotus has been a divine symbol in Asian traditions representing purity. Jute is a long, soft, shiny vegetable fibre that can be spun into coarse, strong threads. Jute is one of the cheapest natural fibres, being second only to cotton in amount produced and variety of uses. The fabric made from jute is popularly known as burlap in North America. Jute is part of Bengali culture, shared by both Bangladesh and West Bengal of India.

Elizabeth and Philip have four children, with Andrew born on February 19, 1960 being the first child to be born to a reigning monarch for 103 years, and Edward born March 10, 1964. All four children have married and produced eight grandchildren for the Queen. She is one of the longest-reigning British monarchs, after Victoria who reigned over the United Kingdom for 63 years, and George III who reigned over Great Britain for 59 years.

In Tudor and Stuart times the kings and queens loved the river and built magnificent riverside palaces at Hampton Court, Kew, Richmond on Thames, Whitehall and Greenwich. Three buildings at Kew, which is now a western suburb of London, have been known as Kew Palace. One of them survives and is a tourist site.

The Royal Botanic Gardens, Kew are extensive gardens and botanical glasshouses, an internationally important botanical research and education institution. The Director of Gardens is responsible for the world's largest collection of living plants. The organization employs more than 650 scientists and other staff. The living collections include more than 30,000 different kinds of plants, while the herbarium has over 7 million preserved plant specimens. The library contains more than 750,000 volumes, and the illustrations collection contains more than 175,000 prints and drawings of plants.

The collections of the British Museum, which number more than seven million objects, are among the largest and most comprehensive in the world and originate from all continents, illustrating and documenting the story of human culture from its beginning to the present. The British Museum was established in 1753, largely based on the collections of the physician and scientist Sir Hans Sloane. The museum first opened to the public on January 15, 1759 in Montagu House in Bloomsbury, on the site of the current museum building.

London's Marble Arch was built in 1827 of white Italian Carrara marble, the design being taken from Rome's triumphal arch of Constantine. The arch once stood at the entrance to Buckingham Palace, but when Queen Victoria enlarged the palace in 1851, she moved it to the entrance of Hyde Park.

Piccadilly Circus is a famous road junction and public space of London's West End in the City of Westminster, built in 1819 to connect Regent Street with the major shopping street of Piccadilly. In this context a *circus*, from the Latin word meaning a circle, is a circular open space at a street junction. As a major traffic-intersection, Piccadilly Circus is a busy meeting place and tourist attraction. The Circus is known for the Shaftesbury memorial fountain and statue of an archer known as *Eros*. It is surrounded by several noted buildings, including the London Pavilion and Criterion Theatre. Directly underneath the plaza is Piccadilly Circus London Underground station.

With its position in the heart of London, Trafalgar Square is one of the most famous squares in the United Kingdom and the world. At its centre is Nelson's Column which was built between 1840 and 1843 to commemorate Admiral Horatio Nelson's death at the Battle of Trafalgar in 1805, a British naval victory of the Napoleonic Wars. The eighteen foot statue of Nelson stands on top of a 151 foot granite column. The statue faces south looking towards the Admiralty (the authority responsible for the command of the Royal Navy), with the Mall (the road running from Buckingham Palace at its western end to Admiralty Arch and on to Trafalgar Square at its eastern end) on his right flank, where Nelson's ships are represented on the top of each flagpole. The top of the Corinthian column is decorated with bronze acanthus leaves cast from British cannon.

The Acanthus is a plant which has come to mean quality, longevity and creativity. The plant, native to Greece, was prized more for its leaves than its beautiful spires of tubular flowers. It first appeared in architecture on the Corinthian Columns of Ancient Greece and is synonymous with Greek architecture. Its name is the Latinized form of the Greek Akanthos (the prefix of which means spiny). Its deeply divided ornate leaves decorated buildings and columns throughout Greek, Roman and medieval times. In renaissance art it is found in sculpture, woodcarvings and friezes.

The square pedestal of Nelson's Column is decorated with four bronze panels, cast from captured French guns, depicting Nelson's four great victories. The Column is guarded by four lion statues at its base.

Dad brought us back to London on the second Saturday in June, the Sovereign's official birthday, to witness the splendid ceremony of Trooping the colour. The custom of Trooping the Colour dates back to the time of Charles II in the 17th Century when the Colours of a regiment were used as a rallying point in battle and were therefore trooped in front of the soldiers every day to make sure that every man could recognize those of his own regiment. Dressed in the uniform of the colonel of the regiment, the King rode along the parade route extending from Buckingham Palace along The Mall to Horse Guards Parade just before Admiralty Arch. There the king took the salute as the scarlet-uniformed, bear-skinned Brigade of Guards (consisting of Grenadier, Coldstream, Scots, Irish and Welsh Guards), together with massed bands, put on a display of precision march (trooping). Over 1400 officers and men are on parade, together with two hundred horses; over four hundred musicians from ten bands and corps of drums march and play as one.

Chapter 9

Seeing the Sites

Dad was eager to introduce us to his family living in Grays. His father, Samuel Robert Todd was born on July 6, 1850 in Cambridgeshire, a county in eastern England. With beautiful countryside and lovely towns and cities, Cambridgeshire is rich in history and boasts the famous Cambridge University, the birthplace of Oliver Cromwell, majestic cathedrals such as Ely Cathedral built in 1083, and magnificent stately homes. Cambridgeshire has ancient abbeys, modern museums such as the Imperial War Museum at Duxford, Britain's foremost aviation museum; old-fashioned breweries; the 17th-century Grantchester vicarage, former home of English poet Rupert Brooke; and the Rupert Brooke Museum. The county is one of the chief cereal and sugar-beet producing districts of England, with other fruits and vegetables also grown; there is dairy farming and sheep-rearing. Cambridgeshire forms part of the Fenlands, which up until the 17th century was mainly marshland. In the 17th century, much of the land was drained for farmland. Although the county is generally very flat, there are hills in the south (the Gog Magog Hills), in the southeast (near Weston Colville, West Wickham, and Castle Camps), and in the west. The hills are mainly boulder clay on top of chalk. The south is more wooded than the rest of the county. It is renowned for its waterways, and most towns can be reached by boat. The monasteries at Thorney and Ramsey were founded before the Norman Conquest. There are outstanding examples of medieval architecture in the county's many fine churches. There are medieval bridges at Huntingdon, Wansford, and St Ives, and important houses at Burleigh, Elton, and Hinchingbrooke.

Samuel Todd's first wife died and then he married Emma Barrett on April 21, 1879 in County Lancaster, Barrow-in-Furness, England. Barrow-in-Furness, known simply as Barrow, is an industrial town and seaport, lying one hundred miles northwest of Manchester. The town is situated at the tip of the Furness peninsula bordered by Morecambe Bay and the Irish Sea. Barrow is located 60 miles south of the Scottish border. The building of the Furness Railway allowed iron ore to be transported to the area; the village's location made it ideal for smelting and then exporting steel. The natural harbour the booming town possessed allowed the locally produced steel to be used for shipbuilding.

Emma Barrett was born on January 2, 1858 in Cambridgeshire, eight years younger than Samuel, from his home area. The Barretts were a gypsy family. The gypsies were an intelligent people, used to living by their wits, and found it easy to impress the uneducated locals by giving themselves unwarranted titles and assuming the importance to go with them. They arrived in Europe as Lords, Dukes, Counts and Earls, demanding and receiving help and support from those in authority. Maybe that's why Emma was called a princess?

Gypsies lived in caravans and cooked their food over campfires. They lived off the generosity of the locals, and when insufficient was forthcoming, helped themselves. The ladies soon gained a reputation as fortune-tellers, but as many of their 'clients' were relieved of their purses at the same time, they also gained the reputation of being thieves and pickpockets. They roamed far and wide, living the nomadic life, with the men carrying on their trades as horse dealers, musicians and workers of metal.

Samuel may have known Emma's family when he was growing up, may have even played with her older brothers—a gypsy camp was a curiosity for youngsters. Samuel and Emma had 13 children, with four of them, including a set of twins, dying as infants. The children living in Grays in 1936 were Violet (Cis), Samuel, Robert, Rose and May.

Grandpa Samuel was a prize fighter in boxing and wrestling and he travelled throughout England for his bouts. Perhaps they travelled in a gypsy caravan, a form of transport that Emma was familiar with. Grandma Emma, as a gypsy princess, danced as part of the entertainment for her husband's boxing bouts and may have done some fortune-telling as well. Samuel was a big man with a 22" neck, a 66" chest and large hands. He was a champion cross-country runner. Samuel was considered one of the toughest men in England and given the nickname Lujia. (Lugia are very large mythical creatures which bear a resemblance to something between a dragon, a reptile and a bird.) In the Grenadier Guards, he set a long jump record with his twenty-two foot jump with a full pack and rifle. Grenadiers were soldiers specially trained to carry and use hand grenades. Particularly tall and strong soldiers were usually picked to become grenadiers because of the weight of extra equipment that they carried.

Samuel loved children and wrote poetry. He lived a long life, dying at the age of 88 years on June 6, 1939 and is buried in Grays. Emma had a soft, becalming voice and she prayed daily for her family. After the death of her husband, Grandma stayed with her daughter Rose, then her daughter Cis, and later lived with us until her death on October 24, 1944, just shy of her 87th birthday.

Aunt Cis married William Thompson, a tall, slender man with wavy hair and well-developed muscles for the lifting required as a dock worker, one of thousands of people employed in international trade, warehousing and related trades in London. Over time, manufacturing industries moved into the Docklands, including large coal and gas plants and storage, the Pura Lard factory, flour mills, and many other businesses. During World War II, the docks area was heavily bombed during the Blitz, in an attempt to cripple the British economy. This destroyed or damaged much of the infrastructure and many older buildings were lost.

Aunt Cis and William had eleven children, several of whom were married with children by the time I met them in 1936—that was quite a large gathering for that one family. William, the oldest son, married Millie and had two sons; Violet married a Scottish fellow; Nellie married Mr. Watts; Thomas married Lily and they had a young son, Ronald; Daisy married Mr. Andrews and they had a son, Ray; Jean, Gwen, Charlie, Ivy and Andrew were younger. I look a lot like Aunt Cis as I grow older; cousin Jean and I looked a lot alike when I met her.

Uncle Sam was married to Violet and they had six children. Samuel was 13, Phylis was 5, with Christopher, Doreen and Doris in between. Joe was the baby born in 1938.

Uncle Robert married Elizabeth Margaret Skeggs and they had six surviving children, William Robert, May, Percival George, Lily, John and Violet. Uncle Bob liked music and could play almost anything by ear. He worked on the London docks like his brother Sam and brother-in-law William. Aunt Elizabeth lost her Mom when she was 13 years old and was put into domestic service when she was 14. She was a good seamstress, and could she cook. I can still taste the roast beef, dumplings and all the trimmings she made on our first visit.

William Robert, the oldest son of Uncle Robert, married Zenieth John and their first child, Zena, was a one-year-old toddler in 1936. May, the oldest daughter of Uncle Robert, was not well when I met her and she died the next year at the young age of 20. Lily was the same age as me—it was nice to have a cousin my age; Lily was killed during the war in 1940. Violet was five years younger than me, being born on February 4, 1925.

Aunt Rose was on her third marriage by the time I met her, being married to John Searles, a coloured man from Jamaica. Aunt Rose had two daughters, Lily and May, from her first marriage to Jim Angus. From her second marriage to Mr. Greenough, she had two sons, Bill and Charlie who worked doing house and road repairs. Aunt Rose and John Searles had two sons, Reggie and Jim. Rose was musical, as were many of the Todd relatives, and she was the proprietor of a music store.

Aunt May was born in 1901 and had jet black, wavy hair. She was 5'4" in height. I was named after her. On October 18, 1921, she married Leonard Bailey, a six-foot tall, good looking man with fair curly hair. They had four surviving children: Leonard Richard was a year younger than me, Clarice May, Dorothea (Dolly) Mavis, and Michael (Micky) were aged about two years apart with Micky arriving in 1929. Leonard did many jobs, such as a road sweeper, on a training ship as a lad, in the docks as an adult, and during the war he was in the merchant navy. Unfortunately for the family, Leonard liked gambling, booze and women.

I started working in December 1935 for Bata Shoe Factory, my first job in England, at the bright young age of 15. It was at Bata that I met Mildred Levitt, who lived in Stanford-le-Hope, a few miles from Grays, and we became good friends. On Saturdays she came over by bus and we went to the show. Other times we went shopping for clothes, sometimes catching a train to West Ham or the ferry to Gravesend. Gravesend is located at a point where the high land of the North Downs reaches the river bank. To the east are the low-lying marshy areas of the Shorne Marshes; to the west, beyond Northfleet, the Swanscombe Marshes. The settlement which grew up was the only good landing place; it was sheltered by the prominent height of what is now called Windmill Hill. In 1401 a Royal Grant was issued, allowing the men of the town to operate boats between London and the town; these became known as the "Long Ferry". It was the preferred form of passage because of the perils of the road journey from highwaymen.

In 1936 we visited our Clayton relatives in Manchester. Mom was the oldest of her sisters and it was a wonderful reunion for her to visit Eliza Jane Clayton Buxton and Mary Clayton Preen in this city of their birth. I met my cousins Louie and Alan Preen and Evelyn Buxton. Evelyn Buxton was married to Ernest Foden on July 15, 1939. I was a bridesmaid at Louie's wedding to Jim Pearson later that summer before the war started. We visited Manchester as often as we could, returning in 1940 to see everyone. In 1941 Mildred and I went to Gorton, Manchester and stayed with Aunt Mary and Louie and Jim Pearson. We had our portraits taken while we were there.

In 1936 we visited with Mom's cousin Ada and husband Harry who lived in Edgeware, Middlesex. He gave me a pair of folding scissors in a leather case which I treasured all of my life.

Liverpool, located on the eastern side of the Mersey Estuary, founded in the year 1207, a major port by the 18th century with trade from the west Indies, Ireland and mainland Europe, with 40% of the world's trade passing through its docks by the early 19th century, and with the popularity of the Beatles, is a tourist attraction which we enjoyed visiting in August 1938.

The Isle of Man is a self-governing Crown dependency located in the Irish Sea at the geographical centre of the British Isles. The head of state is Queen Elizabeth II who holds the title of Lord of Mann. The island is not part of the United Kingdom but foreign relations, defense and ultimate good-governance of the Isle of Man are the responsibility of the government of the United Kingdom. The island is thirty-two miles long and between eight and fifteen miles wide. As well as the main island of Man itself, the Isle of Man includes some nearby small islands: the seasonally inhabited Calf of Maw; Chicken Rock on which stands an unmanned lighthouse; St. Patrick's and St. Michael's Isle, both connected to the mainland by permanent roads/causeways. Hills in the south and north are bisected by a central valley. The majority of sea excursions taken from the Lancashire and North Wales coast resorts were with the two dominant companies in the area. The Liverpool and North Wales Steamship Company in 1890 were using the almost new Fairfield-built St. Tudno (1). The older and smaller steamers were no match for this magnificent paddle steamer.

We walked through the medieval castle in Castletown and learned how it was used for residence, defense, a jail and official offices. We visited the ruined castle on the Isle of St. Patrick hearing tales of vikings, monks, and a ghost dog.

Set upon the hills near the village Laxey rests the great Laxey Wheel known as 'Lady Isabella', named after former Lieutenant Governor Hope's wife. Built in 1854 by John Casement, a Laxey native and talented engineer, the Laxey Wheel is the largest working waterwheel in the world, having a diameter of 72 feet and a circumference of 227 feet. It was used to pump 250 gallons of water a minute from the Laxey mines 200 yards away and 1500 feet below ground. The mines employed over 600 miners at its peak producing lead, copper, silver and zinc till the mines closed in 1929. We were able to climb to the top of the water wheel and view the surrounding countryside from over 70 feet up. We rode on a tram car up the mountain Snaefell. We travelled to Cregneash and visited the village where the people live in thatched cottages, speak the native Manx language, and practice local trades and crafts, living in the manner of those in the past generations, not having changed their way of life with the advancements that society has made.

Blackpool, a seaside town in Lancashire, lying along the coast of the Irish Sea, located 40 miles north-west of the city of Manchester, with the practice of sea-bathing to cure diseases becoming fashionable among the wealthier classes by the middle of the 18th century, and with access by railway, it was an ideal place for our family to spend a week of holidays in August 1938. Three piers were built in Blackpool from 1863 to 1893 and included a theatre, a large open-air dance floor, and opera house, and Blackpool Tower on the promenade. The Golden Mile is the name given to the stretch of Promenade between the North and South piers. In the late 19th Century small-time fairground operators, fortune-tellers and oyster bars were set up in the front gardens of boarding houses to take advantage of passing trade near the railway station. In 1879, Blackpool was the first municipality in the world to have electric street lighting, with large parts of the promenade being wired. The Blackpool Tower, a tourist attraction opened to the public on May 14, 1894, was inspired by the Eiffel Tower in Paris and it rises to 158 metres.

We concluded our vacation in New Brighton. Before the turn of the century, New Brighton, Lancashire had grown into a flourishing seaside resort with the town's excellent beaches attracting day-trippers from the wider Merseyside area and each weekend crowds would pour across the river to enjoy the attractions. New Brighton was easily reached by ferry from Liverpool and the rail links made it an ideal venue for those travelling from Lancashire and Cheshire. One major feature was the New Brighton Tower complex on the north-east tip of the peninsula dominated by the 621 foot high tower, a tower that rivaled the Eiffel Tower in Paris, and was 100 feet higher than the one in Blackpool. Beneath the tower there was a huge circus auditorium capable of seating 3,000 and on the first floor a ballroom with a capacity for 4,500 people. With the grounds containing amusements including a monkey house and an aviary, refreshment rooms, billiard saloons, a Japanese restaurant, a Burmese village complete with Burmese people brought in from near Mandalay, a railway and a cycling and athletics stadium for 80,000 spectators, it was an incredible venture and a huge investment. It was reported in the local press that the Tower Grounds offered the most complete pleasure and recreational resort in the north of England which was made available for the public. During the First World War the tower became unsafe and had to be taken down. The Tower ballroom below remained and hosted many musical events. There was a 62-piece orchestra that attracted the likes of Edward Elgar to conduct. Musical and theatre greats including Gracie Fields, Nellie Melba and Harry Lauder performed here.

In 1939 we travelled to Ramsgate, a seaside town on the Isle of Thanet in east Kent, located seventy-eight miles from central London in an east south easterly direction. Ramsgate's main attraction is its coastline with its main industries being tourism and fishing. The town has one of the largest marinas on the English south coast and Port Ramsgate has provided cross channel ferries for many years. Ramsgate's harbour is a defining characteristic of the town, the construction of which began in 1749 and was completed in 1850. The Harbour is the only Royal Harbour in the United Kingdom. Because of its proximity to mainland Europe, Ramsgate was a chief embarkation point both during the Napoleonic Wars and for the Dunkirk evacuation in 1940. In 1901, the Isle of Thanet saw the introduction of an electric tram service which was one of the few inter-urban tramways in Britain. The towns of Ramsgate, Margate and Broadstairs were linked by 11 miles of track.

During the early part of World War II, I went with Dad and Willie to see our cousins, John and Tarz Todd who were with the Canadian army in Surrey. Tarz also visited us in Grays later on. We also saw cousins Maxwell McKay and John Gynane, children of Mom's sisters Evelyn Clayton McKay and Alice Ann Clayton Gynane. Maxwell rescued a man in a bombed-out building in London. Florence Gynane was in the Canadian Women's Army Corp (CWAC) and she visited us twice, once spending the Christmas holiday with us.

Along with neighbours Ruby Wingham and Dorothy "Bubbles" Dodkin, and Jenny Hounsome, Mildred and I often went to seaside resorts which were easily reached by bus or train. From August 3-10, 1946 we were at Middleton Tower Holiday Camp at Morecambe Bay. Morecambe Bay is a large bay in northwest England, east of the Isle of Man and south of the Lake District National Park. It is the largest expanse of intertidal mudflats and sand in the United Kingdom, covering a total area of 310 square kilometres. The rivers Leven, Kent, Keer, Lune and Wyre drain into the Bay, with their various estuaries making a number of peninsulas within the bay, such as Humphrey Head.

Much of the land around the bay is reclaimed, forming salt marshes used in agriculture. Morecambe Bay is also an important wildlife site, with abundant bird life and varied marine habitats, and there is a bird observatory at Walney Island.

The bay is known for its quicksand and fast moving tides (it is said that the tide can come in "as fast as a horse can run"). There have been royally appointed local guides for crossing the bay for centuries. This difficulty of crossing the bay added to the isolation of the land to its north which, due to the presence of the mountains of the Lake District, could only be reached by crossing these sands or by ferry, until the Furness Railway was built in 1857. This skirts the edge of the bay, crossing the various estuaries.

In the 19th Century the village became popular with visitors to the nearby new huge Middleton Towers Holiday Camp resort of Morecambe and its charms found favour with the holidaymakers from Scotland and Yorkshire. At the height of its popularity, thousands of people were attracted to the District each summer season. Heysham Head is an open expanse of land overlooking Heysham Village and Morecambe Bay with public walkways crossing the area. The Head terminates in cliffs of sandstone.

Towards the end of the last century the Stone Jetty in Morecambe (originally called the Old Pier) operated sailings to Londonderry, Belfast and Dublin. The shallow water and the rise and fall of the tides made it impossible to run a regular boat service. In 1895 plans were drawn up to build Heysham harbour at a cost of £3million and it opened in 1904. One of the Port's great advantages is that it offers immediate access to the sea at all states of the tide.

Southend-on-Sea, a seaside resort in the east of England 40 miles east of central London, has the longest pleasure pier in the world. In the early 19th century, Southend was growing as a resort with people believing that spending time at the seaside was good for their health and with its close proximity to the capital, many Londoners came here. The one drawback was the large mudflats with the sea never being very deep even at full tide and receding for well over a mile at low tide. Large boats were unable to stop at Southend and no boats at all at low tide. Many potential visitors travelled past Southend to go to Margate or other resorts where docking facilities were better. In order to counter this trend, a 600 foot wooden pier based on oak piles was opened in June 1830. It was still too short to be used at low tide, so it was extended to three times its length to 7,000 feet. A railway line reached Southend in the 1850s and made travel here very convenient. The wooden pier was replaced by an iron pier which was completed in stages from 1887 to 1897. An upper deck was added to the pier head in 1907, and the pier was extended further in 1927 to accommodate larger steamboats. In August 1946, Mildred and I spent a holiday there. I returned the following summer with Ethel and Pat Driscoll and May Smith as my travelling companions and got my best tan in all twelve years that I was in England.

In 1946, Mom, Dad, Willie, Aunt Mary and I visited Clacton-on-Sea, the largest town on the Tendring Peninsula in Essex, a seaside resort attracting many tourists, being served by a railway line only 90 minutes away from London. Clacton has a pleasure pier, arcades, a golf course, caravan parks and an airfield. The town and its beaches remain popular with tourists in the summer.

A group of the girls spent a day at Lancaster Castle, an ancient castle, a Crown Court and a Category C men's prison located on the Lune River in north west England in Lancaster. In 1086, Roger de Poitou, a relative of William the Conqueror, started building the castle. King John is said to have held court at Lancaster Castle. Many famous trials and executions have happened at the Castle with the first trial being held in 1196. There were more death sentences handed down at Lancaster Castle than any other Court in England, except Old Newgate in London. More people were executed for forgery than for any other offence. There were two hundred separate offences that carried the death penalty until 1825. The age of criminal responsibility, when you were subject to adult sentences, including the death penalty, was nine years old—can you imagine that? We have come a long ways since then. Crowds of thousands of people used to come to watch public executions outside the Castle. From 1614 until the war of independence, some offenders were deported to America, while later offenders were deported to Australia, with a total of 200,000 people being deported from Lancaster. Hadrian's

Tower, an old prison no longer in use, is situated at the centre of the old Roman cavalry fort, with the walls being nine and a half feet thick. The Shire Hall was opened in 1800 and is still used to try civil law cases. The other court is the Crown Court which is the oldest working court room in Britain. In 1812 there were 512 prisoners in Lancaster Castle, while today the maximum is 240. Lancaster Castle is owned by the Duke of Lancaster who is also the reigning monarch.

The Doone Valley is one of the most picturesque places on Exmoor. The name derives from one of the great mythical persons of Exmoor, Lorna Doone. "Lorna Doone—A Romance of Exmoor" is a novel by Richard Doddridge Blackmore first published in 1869 and has never been out of print. The book is set in the 17th century in the region of Exmoor in Devon and Somerset. John Ridd is the son of a respectable farmer who was murdered in cold blood by a member of the notorious Doone clan, a once-noble family now living in the Doone Valley. Battling his desire for revenge, John also grows into a respectable farmer and continues to take good care of his mother and two sisters. He falls hopelessly in love with Lorna, a girl he meets by accident, who turns out to be not only the granddaughter of Sir Ensor Doone (lord of the Doones), but destined to marry (against her will) the impetuous, menacing and now jealous heir of the Doone Valley, Carver Doone. Carver will let nothing get in the way of his marriage to Lorna, which he plans to force upon her once Sir Ensor dies and he comes into his inheritance. Having read the book about Lorna Doone, I always wanted to go to the Doone Valley but my early return to Canada forestalled this trip. Mildred visited it and sent me pictures, the next best thing to being there.

Chapter 10

Where Are You?

Britain was blacked out on September 1, 1939, two days before war broke out. A blackout is when the lights are turned off in a city so that enemy bombers cannot see any recognizable sites that would help them to know where to release their bombs. Everyone had to cover their windows and doors at night with heavy blackout curtains, cardboard or paint. Street lights were switched off or dimmed and shielded to deflect the light downward. Traffic lights and vehicle headlights were fitted with slotted covers to deflect their beams down to the ground. Thousands of people died in road accidents because of the lack of street lighting and the dimmed traffic lights. To help prevent accidents, white stripes were painted on the roads and lamp-posts. People were encouraged to walk facing the traffic and men were encouraged to leave their shirt-tails hanging out so that they could be seen by cars with dimmed headlights. We still have white lines painted on our roads and we still walk facing the traffic, always interesting where today's practices originated. The blackout was total by the end of September 1939—no chink of light was permitted to show.

People were injured during the blackout because they could not see in the darkness. They were injured tripping up stairs, falling down stairs, or bumping into things. Most Luftwaffe air raids took place at night. To protect their planes from fighter planes, and the heavy artillery below, the German pilots flew thousands of feet above the ground. The blackout made it hard for the Germans to find and hit their targets.

The benefits of a blackout against air attack are now largely nullified with the invention, as early as World War II, of aircraft using radio beam navigation, and targets were detected by air-to-ground radar. Today night-vision goggles are readily available to air crews, as well as sophisticated satellite-based navigation systems enabling a static target to be found easily by aircraft and guided missiles. During the battle of the Atlantic in World War II, German U-boats were greatly aided with the sinking of unescorted ships in American coastal waters because ships were backlit by coastal lights. In any naval war, this would still be an advantage that a blackout would help to nullify.

The appearance of German bombers in the skies over London during the afternoon of September 7, 1940 showed a shift in Hitler's attempt to subdue Britain. During the previous two months, the Luftwaffe had targeted Royal Air Force airfields and radar stations in preparation for Germany's invasion of the island. These bombing raids on London were an attempt to demoralize the people and force the British to come to terms. At 4 p.m. on September 7, 348 German bombers escorted by 617 fighters blasted London for two hours. Two hours later, guided by the fires set by the first assault, a second group of raiders began another attack that lasted until 4:30 in the morning. This was the beginning of the Blitz, with intense bombing of London and other cities that continued for eight months. For fifty-seven consecutive days, London was bombed either during the day or night. Fires consumed many parts of the city. Residents sought shelter wherever they could find it with many fleeing to the Underground train stations.

We lived in fear for our lives, day after day, night after night, our ears ringing from the air raid sirens and the noise of the bombs exploding. We never knew if we would survive another attack, but despite that, we carried on with our daily lives, going to work to keep the economy going, to provide needed goods and services. At any time of the day or night, the air raid sirens would sound the alarm and we would head to the nearest shelter. Anderson air raid shelters were issued free to families earning less than £250 a year. The steel-built, tunnel-shaped shelters were made in sections which had to be assembled. Dad installed one at the bottom of our garden in Grays Essex. It was partly sunk into the ground and then covered with dirt. It measured 6 feet 6 inches by 4 feet 6 inches. Rhubarb was planted beside it, as part of the camouflage. Dad built a wooden overhang by the door.

Chapter 11

This is a Plane?

Canada joined the war efforts on September 10, 1939. This was a week after Britain joined due to the Statute of Westminster, requiring Canada to vote before entering a war. With the war going on in Europe and Asia, Canada didn't have any major problems in manufacturing supplies for the war other than switching factories to make war equipment. Many factories were set up which helped increase the employment rate. Canada was one of the largest trainers of pilots for the Allies. Many Canadian men joined the war efforts, so with the men overseas and industries pushing to increase production, women took up positions to aid in the war effort.

During war many supplies were needed and there was a low supply of goods. Women took the initiative to recycle and salvage in order to come up with needed supplies. They gathered recycled goods, handed out information on the best methods to use so that they could get the most out of recycled goods, and organized other events to decrease the amount of waste. Volunteer organizations led by women prepared packages for the military overseas or for prisoners of war in Axis countries.

With World War II and the great need for employees in the workplace, without women to step in the economy would have collapsed. By autumn 1944 the number of women working full-time in Canada's paid labour force was twice what it had been in 1939, between 1,000,000 and 1,200,000, not including part-time workers or women working on farms. Women worked these intensive labour jobs and they still had to find time to make jams, clothes and other acts of volunteering to aid the men overseas.

In 1916 in the First World War, Germany started using its submarines to sink ships that were bringing food to the country to starve Britain into surrender. Within two years, Britain had just six weeks of food left and had to ration its food supplies.

At the beginning of World War II, the United Kingdom was importing 55 million tons of foodstuffs per year, which was 70% of the country's needs, including more than 50% of its meat, 70% of its cheese and sugar, 80% of fruits, and 90% of cereals and fats. It was one of the principal strategies of the Axis powers to attack shipping bound for the United Kingdom, restricting British industry and potentially starving the nation into submission. To deal with extreme shortages, a system of rationing was introduced very early in the war. By January 1940, bacon, butter and sugar were rationed, followed by meat, tea, jam, biscuits, breakfast cereals, cheese, eggs, milk and canned fruit. One of the few foods not rationed were fish and chips. As the war progressed, most kinds of food were rationed, as were clothing and gasoline. Fruits and fresh vegetables were not rationed as they would spoil. Families grew victory gardens of vegetables, fruits and herbs at their homes to reduce the pressure on the public food supply. Making victory gardens became a part of daily life on the home front. People in the countryside were less affected by rationing as they had greater access to locally sourced unrationed products than people in metropolitan areas.

Rationing continued after the end of the war and even became stricter. Bread, which was not rationed during the war, was rationed form 1946 to 1948; and potato rationing began in 1947. This was largely due to the necessity of feeding the population of European areas coming under British control whose economies had been devastated by the fighting. Sweet rationing ended in February 1953, and sugar rationing ended in September. The end of all food rationing did not come until July 4, 1954, with meat and bacon the last to go.

From very early in the war, it was thought that the major industrial cities of Britain, especially London in the south east, would come under Nazi German Luftwaffe air attack, which did happen with The Blitz. Some children were sent to Canada, the USA and Australia and millions of children and some mothers were evacuated from London and other major cities when the war began, and more were evacuated during The Blitz bombing which began in September 1940. Children were evacuated if their parents agreed but in some cases they did not have a choice. The children were only allowed to take a few things with them, including a gas mask, books, money, clothes, ration book and some small toys.

On March 17, 1941 there was a call from the Minister of Labour, Ernest Bevin, for 100,000 to do war work in the factories. Registration of twenty and twenty-one year old women began the next month, with the aim of filling vital jobs in industry and the auxiliary services. One of the prime targets was to get shell-filling factories working round the clock. Women were desperately needed to take over all kinds of other jobs to free men for active service. Married women with young children were exempt.

I was called up and worked on war work in Chelmsford, Essex making parts for fans, motors, etc. I wanted to work at something to do with building airplanes, but nothing that I did "looked like an airplane." This town received much bombing because of the many factories there. Where I boarded they had a Morrison indoor air raid shelter. It was like a big iron table which replaced the dining table. The top and legs were iron and there was a wire mesh around the sides. When the air raid siren sounded, we crawled under it.

While I was living away from home, my landlady taught me to knit. I made mitts, gloves and sweaters—partly to prove to Dad that I could knit. He was quite pleased with the sweater I brought home for Mom that I knitted myself. I was fortunate in being able to get home by bus every Saturday afternoon and return Sunday evening. My neighbours Ruby and Bubbles also came to work in Chelmsford and the three of us travelled together.

My mother was sick off and on and Dad tried to get my release from war work to look after her. I did get it and was able to look after Mom by working closer to home. I worked in Grays, Essex at Drums Ltd. from early 1945 to 1946, making steel drums—soldering with gas and electric. When the war was over, the men returned to their former jobs and we had to be transferred or get another job. I went to work at the Board Mills in Purfleet, Essex where we made cardboard cartons, some corrugated—glued the corrugated part to the cardboard; stapled boxes on a sewing machine; counted and tied bundles.

I saw an advertisement for girls to be trained as telephonists and receiving pay as well. Thinking far ahead about maybe one day being able to transfer to Grays telephone exchange, I immediately set out for Faraday House in London, and began training. A great crowd of girls had the same idea but most, if not all, were taken on. We worked in front of a big switchboard.

There were three shifts: 7 a.m. to 3 p.m. one week, 3 p.m. to 11 p.m. the next, then every sixth week we worked the night shift 11 p.m. to 7 a.m.

The Faraday building was the General Post Office's first telephone exchange, opening for business in London on March 1, 1902 with 200 subscribers. The General Post Office (GPO) was officially established in England in 1660 by Charles II and it grew to combine the functions of both the state postal system and telecommunications carrier. The GPO was a monopoly covering the dispatch of items from a specific sender to a specific receiver. The postal service was known as the Royal Mail because it was built on the distribution system for royal and government documents.

When new forms of communication came into existence in the 19th and early 20th centuries the GPO claimed monopoly rights on the basis that like the postal service they involved delivery from a *sender* to a *receiver*. The theory was used to expand state control of the mail service into every form of electronic communication possible. This applied to telegraph and telephone switching stations.

The GPO played a vital role during the Second World War in keeping communication links available for the Government and the armed forces. GPO engineers were responsible for providing the command and control facilities of RAF Fighter Command running throughout the Battle of Britain. In common with other exchanges in London, Central was able to connect subscribers to the Electrophone exchange at Gerard Street. Electrophone allowed people to listen to performances at some London theatres and music halls while sitting at home. In 1933, Faraday became the telephone centre of the world with the opening of the international telephone exchange. In 1935, an automatic exchange was opened with more than 6,000 working lines.

I was working at Faraday House in London the day Princess Elizabeth married Philip Mountbatten. Our supervisor picked names out of a box and these workers were allowed to go to see the wedding procession. Unfortunately I had to work. It wasn't very busy at the exchange during the time of the wedding and we were able to plug into a line and listen to the wedding ceremony.

Just around the corner from where I worked was St. Paul's Cathedral. We were able to tour the building during our lunch break.

I enjoyed the work and met some very nice girls there, and also gained some experience travelling by trains and finding my way around. We got tickets to see "The Ink Spots" and "Lena Horne".

Chapter 12

First Love

How many times a day I wondered why I had decided to leave Mom and Dad and Willie in England and make this trip back alone. What was the urgency? Why couldn't I wait? I had just trained as a telephonist and had a good job. What urged me to give it all up and come back to Canada? What was I looking for in Canada that I didn't have in England? I never liked the dull, damp weather of England, but was that enough to make me step out on my own? I didn't have a boy friend in England and none to go back to in Canada. Was it something Rosa wrote in a letter that encouraged me to return to my homeland? What was it like in England after the war? Lots of rebuilding had to be done. Many bombed out buildings, still rationing. In Canada on the farm there was plenty to eat. Was I tired of Spam and looked forward to some chicken? Was I drooling for a fresh egg?

When I decided to return to Canada in 1948, the girls bought me a going away gift. It was such a surprise, I cried. What might it be? A watch? A necklace? A sweater or blouse? Perfume? Hand lotion? Bath salts? Makeup? I had to open it to find out.

Willie gave me a camera for my 28th birthday on February 23 so that I could send pictures to those remaining in England. It was sad saying goodbye to Mom at home. Aunt Mary from Manchester was with us, staying with Mom while Dad and Willie took me to the train station in Grays and travelled with me to London. There I switched trains to go on to Southhampton on my own. On this train, I met a girl in the washroom who had just said goodbye to her father and brother, both of us were crying.

She was a war bride on her way to Montreal. We boarded the ship Catania on February 26 and spent time together during the trip across the ocean. After boarding, I was surprised to hear my name called over the intercom system. Upon answering the call, I received a "Bon Voyage" telegram from my friends at the telephone exchange in London. The girls really wished me well. Again I thought to myself, why am I leaving? But I was stubborn, I had decided to go and I was on the ship and on my way.

The journey on the ship lasted five days with arrival in Halifax, Nova Scotia, Canada on March 1, 1948. The ship was used as a transport ship for the soldiers during the war and had not yet been converted back to a pleasure ship. There were no cabins; it was a big room with many bunks and only partial partitioning, not like a luxury liner cruise ship of today, just the basics. Once again, I had a top bunk.

From Halifax, I took a train to Toronto where my cousin Bob Todd met me and I stayed overnight with him and his wife Ellen; their daughter Sylvia remembers my visit. I went to stay with cousin Rosa Saillian, sister of Bob, at R.R. #1, Hillsburg, near the village of Ospringe. Rosa and Carl had three children by this time, Bill, Ronald, and Gilbert. Carl had sold his rug business in Toronto; he worked the farm and worked at Gilson Manufacturing in Guelph, making refrigerators. I stayed for awhile on the farm helping with the haying during the summer. Carl took us for drives in the car to such places as Rockwood, Lake Belwood, and Everton.

In April 1948, I started work at Sterling Rubber in Guelph, sorting, checking quality, and packing gloves. At first Carl brought me back and forth to Guelph every day when he came into work. When he was on holidays for a week, I boarded in town. I decided to look for a place to live in Guelph. Mrs. Cromwell rented a semi-detached house at 9 Birmingham Street and she was renting out rooms. I boarded there and continued to work at Sterling Rubber. I met Mrs. Cromwell's son, Oliver, in the fall of 1948 when he came home for a visit from northern Ontario where he had been working. We began dating. We had a picnic at Puslinch Lake for one of our outings.

Oliver and I were married on February 26, 1949 and continued living in Guelph at his mother's place.

> Wedding notice: A quiet wedding took place recently at the home of Elder F. Maclean, when May, daughter of Mr. and Mrs. William Todd, Grays, Essex, England, became the bride of Oliver, son

of Mrs. D. Cromwell, 9 Birmingham Street, Guelph. The bride wore a powder blue two piece dress, with accessories to match, corsage of red roses, and a double strand of pearls, the gift of the groom. She was attended by her cousin, Mrs. Rosa Saillian, as matron of honor, wearing a gray crepe dress with corsage of red carnations. The groom was attended by Mr. Carl Saillian as best man. A reception was held at the home of the groom's mother, who received her guests in a gray crepe dress with corsage of pink carnations. The gift to the matron of honor was a gold locket and to the best man a gold cigarette case. For travelling the bride donned a gray coat with fox trim and navy blue accessories. Mr. and Mrs. Cromwell will reside in Guelph. Gerry Robillard and Doris Cromwell (sister of the groom) also attended (they married later in the year).—Guelph Mercury

Oliver was working in Toronto when James Oliver was born on July 29, 1949. My mother and father arrived from England and surprised me by stopping off to visit, before going to Vancouver where they would live next door to Dad's brother Dick. Just after they arrived, my water broke and labour pains began. I phoned the doctor and he advised me to go to the hospital. I left Mom and Dad at my place until Oliver came home that night and took them to Rosa and Carl's farm for a week. When I came out of hospital, I went to the Saillians with the baby to spend time with Dad and Mom before they left for the West.

I bought a rock-o-roll to use as a rocker, a bed, and a high chair before I left Guelph. All my children have used it.

Oliver's job finished in Toronto and he heard there was work in Winnipeg, Manitoba. He went alone to find a job and a place to live, and then sent for Jim and me. He had rented two upstairs rooms on Main Street. I used a wooden washing machine while there because that was the only kind they could buy during the war. We received a telegram telling us that my mother had died in Vancouver on November 20, 1949. I was really thankful to have had the week to spend with her with her first grandson in August. How many times over the years have I wished I could ask Mom a question, or share something with her.

There was no work with the steel company, so Oliver went to work on a dairy farm in Fort Garry, south of Winnipeg. We moved next door to his work and lived with Leah Dunn. The two upstairs rooms were ours.

Dad left Vancouver and visited us in Fort Garry on his way back to Ontario. He lived on the farm with Carl and Rosa until he got a job at the hospital in Guelph. He moved to Guelph, living at the hospital, and met Anastasia Stokes, who also worked there. They were married on October 7, 1950 and lived at 214 King Street, with subsequent moves to Gordon Street and to 23 Birmingham Street.

My brother Willie was married on March 25, 1950 in England to Joan Lillian Rudd. Although Willie had intended to return to Canada to live, his plans changed with his marriage to an English girl. He lived for the remainder of his life in the land across the ocean from his homeland.

R.M.S. Alaunia—ship taken to England in 1936

May Todd in England

May's parents, Aunt Mary Preen, Louie Preen & Jim Pearson, May Todd

Wedding picture of Oliver Lloyd Cromwell and May Todd Feb 26, 1949

Wedding of May Todd Cromwell and Orlin Elwood Stewart April 16, 1969

Oliver with baby Donald, Grandpa and Grandma Todd, Barbara and James—1953

Ann and William Todd, May's Dad and stepmother.

The combined family April 16, 1969—James, Don, May & Orlin, Cleason, Rodney, Shirley, Bill, Barbara

May and Orlin at Barbara's wedding August 13, 1972.

The Cromwells James, Barbara, Don, May, Shirley, William—1991

William, Barbara, Shirley, James, May, Don—2000

Willie and May Todd—1987

Chapter 13

Water, Water Everywhere and Small Golden Coins No More

In 1950 the Red River climbed to its highest level since 1861, resulting in a major flood from April to June. Snowmelt waters from the United States flow north through a wide, flat plain and severe flooding can create havoc in many small communities as well as in the city of Winnipeg. There had been heavy autumn rains followed by a long winter with great amounts of snow. A cold spring prevented thawing; masses of thick ice deposited on the river caused it to reach flood levels by April 22. Significant rainfall in early May kept the river above flood stage for 51 days. The swirling river, rising northward from Minnesota, turned 600 square miles of Manitoba farmland, between the American border and Winnipeg, into a vast inland sea.

As we watched each day, the water came closer to the dairy farm where Oliver worked and to the house where we lived upstairs. We stayed as long as we could. From May 1 to 5 the water inched higher by the hour, invading the streets and buildings of Winnipeg. On the blustery night of "Black Friday," May 5, during torrential rain, sleet and snow, the powerful Red River tore apart eight dikes, crumpling countless sandbag bastions. Four of Winnipeg's eleven bridges were destroyed, and homes were engulfed. We had to be taken out in a rowboat early the next morning, down the Pembina Highway, Jim's first boat ride. I was moved twice that day, then Oliver decided to send me back to Rosa Saillian's on the farm in Ontario until the flood was over. The cows from the dairy farm were moved to the University of Manitoba.

On May 18 the Red River reached 30.3 feet above normal. Although 107,000 people had been evacuated from the area, Lawson Alfred Ogg was the only Winnipegger killed by the 1950 flood that drowned the city. The disastrous flood caused the city to institute flood control measures with the construction of a large flood-diversion channel, the Red River Floodway. The value of this channel was amply demonstrated in 1997. The catastrophic flood in the spring of that year was caused by snowfall in the neighbouring United States that was 300% above normal and 200% above normal in southern Manitoba. This unusually high accumulation of snow fell on top of ground that was still saturated from the previous autumn. Some 1,950 square kilometers were flooded, including 2,500 homes and about 30,000 people were evacuated. A massive flood-fighting operation, assisted by the Canadian Armed Forces and many volunteers, was mounted. These efforts, and the Red River Floodway, saved Winnipeg from being flooded. Had this effort not succeeded, floodwaters in Winnipeg would have been one metre above the 1950 level. There have been serious floods in 1966, 1979, 1997 and in 2009.

One of the main reasons for staying put as long as we could was Oliver's concern for me as I was near the end of my pregnancy. About one week after arriving in Ontario, on May 23, I gave birth to premature identical twin girls. Linda died on May 24th, only one day old; I never saw her. I saw Louise once in an incubator, and then Carl Saillian took her in his car, with a nurse, to Toronto Sick Children's Hospital; she died on May 30th. After carrying the babies for nearly nine months, it was heart-breaking to lose both of them within a week. I didn't know I was going to have twins—the medical care I had received was not up to today's standards. Ultra sounds were unknown at this time, only being introduced to the medical world in the 1960s. Ultrasound was invented by the English physician Ian Donald in 1957 and the following year it was used on a pregnant woman for the first time. Sound waves of very high frequencies can easily and harmlessly penetrate human flesh. As waves enter the body, they encounter different materials such as bone and internal organs. These materials cause the waves to reflect back to the source. Because the waves reflect back differently, a physician can identify the type of tissue by the nature of the reflection. Without the invention of the ultrasound device, doctors wouldn't be able to view the fetus of a woman and even see internal organs and bones that could save lives or help prevent damages. Ultrasound has become the second most widely-used diagnostic imaging modality today.

It took me awhile to adjust to the fact that my babies were gone. What did I do wrong that my babies died? Did I not eat right? Was that chocolate cake the wrong thing to eat? Was it that one glass of wine? Children are not supposed to die. The girls were my hope for the future. Part of me died on May 24 and another part on May 30th. My pouch of gold coins was feeling the loss of these two little ones. Every year from then on the month of May was a tough one, dealing with the sadness. I never forgot Linda and Louise. On Mother's Day later on, I had five other golden coins, but the two that were wrenched away so early were always remembered with a little sadness. My heart still cries out for them. I have memories of them moving in the womb, but one quick look at Louise didn't provide much of a memory to hold close over the next few days and weeks. My arms ached to hold my two little girls. Jimmie got many extra tight hugs when I was feeling especially lonesome. Oliver was so far away that I didn't have his shoulders to cry on. I had to do my crying once Jimmie was asleep. The gift of those two golden coins was a gift I was forced to give up before I had a chance to develop any memories. Two branches, mere twigs, from our family tree were broken off, leaving a gaping hole and a lopsided tree.

I wonder if Linda would have had light brown hair and whether it would have been curly or straight. Did she have blue eyes or hazel like mine? Would she have been a happy, easy-going child with lots of love to share? Would she have been the feisty one because of her slower start in life? Would Louise have had curly dark hair? What would have been the distinguishing mark between the girls? Louise lived longer so she was probably the one who got the most nourishment in the womb. She would likely have been taller.

Would I have been able to tell them apart? Would Oliver have been able to tell them apart? What pretty dresses I would have been able to make for them! Would Linda look better in blue? Would Louise be a beautiful girl in pink? Would the girls be wonderful companions for each other? Would Linda finish sentences that Louise started? Would Louise be able to sense when Linda was in trouble and come running, or call her on the phone? Would Linda become a nurse and care for those in need? Would Louise become a scientist and discover the reason behind things? Would Linda grow to favour me in character, a more sociable person? Would Louise become more like Oliver, shy, a loner, but a very good worker? Would they get along well with their older brother, Jimmie? Jimmie just turned 10 months old—it would have been tough to have two more babies to look after but I was young and looked forward to another child.

The ups and downs of grieving were like a roller coaster. I started off the day fully accepting my loss, and then out of the blue there was that speeding dip down the hillside and the sharp wrench around the curve. Another day I would start at the curve and then Jimmie would do something to make me laugh and I would be cruising on the level track again. But then would come that nagging guilt—I shouldn't be happy when I have just lost Linda and Louise. I was the survivor and had the long, lonely road to travel—no gold coins in my hands or my arms. They burst from my body and then were taken away with barely a glimpse to carry me through the years. If I were to get pregnant again, would I lose that baby too? Is Oliver grieving in Manitoba like I am here in Ontario? He was so looking forward to a second child. It was so sad for me to have to tell him that I had given birth to twins and then the next day tell him that Linda had died. I was crying and he was quiet on the other end of the phone. He will not likely talk about it; he keeps a lot of things inside. On May 30 it was even more heart wrenching to tell Oliver that our second little gold coin, Louise, had also died. For the past several months we talked about the baby. Would it be a girl, or another boy? We expected the baby to be healthy and live a good life. The baby was a reality to us before birth. We had purchased a few newborn clothes—most of Jimmie's baby clothes were still in good shape from the year before. I even bought a pink nightgown in case I had a little girl—I hoped it would be a girl and then I would have one of each. I bonded with the baby throughout the pregnancy. The birth was easy because the twins were both small. Linda weighed 2½ pounds and Louise was just over 3 pounds.

I feel less than whole—something is missing. Oh to smell the newborn baby smell! Oh to hold that small weight in my arms! I understand in my mind that the babies were not healthy and it was better that they died quickly. But my heart aches and says why? Maybe God will use me as their mother when He raises Linda and Louise up from the dead. What a thrill that will be when the graves are opened!

I must get through one day at a time. I must not neglect Jimmie. He is an active baby, crawling all over, pulling himself up on the furniture. Soon he will be walking. I will take him out to the backyard for a swing ride. Carl put a swing up for Jimmie. Carl and Rosa have been a wonderful support to me. I hate to leave them, but, it has been a month since Louise died. For the past three weeks I was feeling so tired. This week I have had more energy. The waves of pain are beginning to ease. It is time for Jimmie and I to make the train trip back to Manitoba.

I returned to Fort Garry in the summer and soon after Oliver got a job with Horton Steel Company again and we moved back into Winnipeg. I liked that city except for the corner of Portage and Main in wintertime. Boy was it ever windy and cold! Winnipeg was incorporated in 1873 with a population of only 1,869. It is situated at the confluence of the Red and Assiniboine rivers, forty miles south of Lake Winnipeg, and sixty miles north of the United States border, midway between the Atlantic and Pacific Oceans. Winnipeg, the capital of Manitoba, had a population of over 243,000 in 1959.

Barbara Jean was born in Winnipeg on September 22, 1951. Our landlord, Mr. Chipourra, took me to the hospital. He said it was the first time he had ever taken anyone else's wife to have her baby. They had five children of their own. Oliver left for Moose Jaw, Saskatchewan one week before Barbara was born. He expected to be away for two months.

> Birth Announcement written to my brother: weight 7 lbs. 12 oz. Dear Willie and Joan, Just a line to say I'm feeling fine after my ordeal. Glad it's all over. I sure have a chubby little girl and she's definitely a Todd. She has lots of jet black hair. It was tough luck that Oliver had to leave for Moose Jaw, Saskatchewan, exactly a week before the baby was born. He only expects to be away for two months. Jimmy is being looked after by Mrs. Dunn at Fort Garry, where we lived before the flood. Well that's all for now. I expect to be home by Saturday or Sunday next. Bye for now. Love, May.

Oliver returned to take us to Saskatchewan. Enroute to Moosejaw, we stopped off in Milestone, in January 1952, for a couple of days to visit Oliver's brother Don and his wife Lil. The brothers had not seen each other for a long time. Don worked on oil rigs. We stayed with them at the only hotel in town. There were no flush toilets, only a big pail with a toilet seat on it. We brought water into our room and used a china wash bowl. Some hotel!!

Oliver had rented rooms for us in Boharm, seven or eight miles outside of Moosejaw. It was winter time and very cold there. The lady of the house had forgotten to warn me about a door leading upstairs to the attic. That was where I hung clothes to dry. If the door closed behind you, it would lock itself. Well, it happened to me! Jimmy and I went up to hang clothes, Barbara was asleep in the buggy in the kitchen, and the people downstairs were away. We were locked in the attic! I didn't know what to do, but fortunately a visitor came to their house that day. I saw him arrive through the attic window and I tried to catch his attention; he did not see me. However, the door was unlocked so he came in. I called to let him know we were locked in the attic, and he came upstairs to let us out. Were we ever happy!

Oliver's job finished in Moosejaw and we had to move again. Every time we moved it was necessary to get rid of more things that were not essential. To the oldest girl at this house I gave my scrapbook on "The Dionne Quintuplets" and one of Movie Stars that I had collected over the years.

We were late getting to the station, but they held up the train for us. Once again we were headed for the Saillians in Ontario, only this time they had moved from the farm to their home on Stevenson Street in Guelph where Carl started up his own rug cleaning business. Barbara got an A-shaped scar on her forehead when she got excited in her play and banged her head against a hot-water radiator.

We took Dad and Ann with us to Elora Gorge, Puslinch Lake and Rockwood in 1952. The grandparents enjoyed spending time with their grandchildren. Oliver also took us to Eden Mills Cemetery where his maternal grandparents, John and Martha Ann Stevenson, were buried.

In 1952 Oliver was called to what was supposed to be four years of work in Sarnia. Actually it only lasted for a little over one year. Horton Steel was building spheres for Imperial Oil Company.

We sub-let the upstairs rooms in a house on Rose Street. Oliver built shelves in the kitchen, built the back stoop, and a sandbox for Jim and Barbara to play in. He put up a new clothesline just in time for our new baby.

Donald Gordon was born in Sarnia on March 27, 1953. This was the first time Oliver was home when I had our babies and was able to take me to the hospital. We lived on Rose Street. Our landlady who lived on the main floor of the house looked after Jim and Barbara while I was in hospital.

Thursday, May 21, 1953 started out as a typical, lovely spring day. The weather forecast was fine weather, but by 2:00 p.m. the sky became overcast and a storm moved in. For the next few hours conditions got worse, and around 5:00 p.m. there was a devastating hail storm. We saw the large hailstones falling as we looked out the window. At 5:42 p.m. the worst tornado ever to strike in Canada up to that time tore a half-kilometre path through the heart of downtown Sarnia.

Only a few minutes after the tornado swept through the city, the sun broke out over the scene of destruction. Over 250 buildings, including

154 houses, were damaged by the tornado. The city lost a lot of trees which were uprooted by the storm. The Vendome Hotel, the Imperial Bank, Taylor's Furniture Store, and the Imperial Theatre were among the most prominent of Sarnia's landmarks damaged. Although 38 victims were treated for injuries sustained in the tornado, miraculously no one was killed in the disaster. About an hour after the tornado hit, cranes and crews from local industries came in to begin the cleanup operations. More that $5,000,000 damage was caused by the tornado which left dozens of families homeless. After supper we went uptown and viewed the damage that had occurred.

Our next move was to Guelph, where we lived a short time with Rosa again. Oliver was sick with pleurisy while there. Pleurisy is an inflammation of the body cavity that surrounds the lungs. Infections are the most common cause of pleurisy. The inflamed pleural layers rub against each other every time the lungs expand to breathe in air. This can cause sharp pain when breathing. In order to drain the fluids in the lungs, a chest tube is inserted and left in place for several days. Usually the patient is in hospital during this time. Antibiotics are prescribed if there is an infection, and lots of rest is required.

After his recovery, Oliver worked in Whitby and came home on the weekends. Shirley May was born in Guelph on June 20, 1954. Rosa looked after the three children while I was in the hospital. Soon after this we moved to a house in the country, near Aberfoyle, on busy Highway #6. Jim and Barbara were old enough to play outside by themselves but when I put Don out in the playpen he screamed and screamed. He didn't like being fenced in! When I took him out of it, I found him heading off up the lane towards the highway. Obviously it was not convenient to continue living there.

I got rooms on Gordon Street, two doors from where Dad and Ann lived, close to Royal City Park. In the fall of 1954, Oliver found us a house to rent in Moffat. There was room for a vegetable garden and lots of flowers. Tulips, daffodils and lily of the valley were colourful in the spring.

Oliver worked for a short time for Percy Robillard in Quebec, and then continued working for Horton Steel there, in Chicoutimi, and in New Brunswick, only getting home on long holiday weekends.

Because Oliver was away so much of the time, Shirley became upset when he came home. She used to cling to me and didn't want me to put her down. I thought he would have quite a time with her while I was in town shopping, but he made her a swing and everything worked out well.

Chapter 14

Oh the Anguish

August 8, 1955 a hot, sunny Monday, a perfect day for hanging the washing out on the line. Lots of washing for a family with four children!

After the washing was blowing in the light breeze, it was time to pick some fresh vegetables for supper. Tomatoes, green beans, new potatoes, cucumbers and even a few carrots would sure taste delicious tonight! Just a little salt, pepper and butter—yum, yum. I also dug up enough beets to fill my large pot to make pickled beets—I would be sure to save a few out for supper. The sand was removed, the beet tops cut off and water was added and they were put on to boil—I was using the stove in the basement. Pickled beets were a favourite of the children and ourselves. I had the radio playing quietly and had just heard the number one song on the charts, "Rock Around the Clock" by Bill Haley and His Comets—I often sang along to the songs on the radio.

Jimmie was playing quietly upstairs in the living room while Barbara, Donnie and Shirley were having their afternoon naps.

Roy Campanella was featured on the cover of Time Magazine today. Campanella is an American baseball player, considered to be one of the greatest catchers in the history of the game. Campanella played for the Brooklyn Dodgers during the 1940s and 1950s, as one of the pioneers in breaking the colour barrier in Major League Baseball. I saw the magazine when I made a quick trip to the corner store this morning when we went for a short walk after the washing was hanging on the line.

The weather in Britain this month has been very warm and sunny. It reminds me of the one year when I was in England that I got a beautiful tan. The Bank Holiday Monday was a beautiful day. They are predicting even better weather as the month of August progresses. It was even hot in Scotland.

The Atomic Energy Conference opened in Geneva today with Dr. Homi Bhabha as President. It is said to be a unique gathering which may have a far-reaching effect on the development of the world. For the first time in history leading scientists and technologists from all lands whose special function is to penetrate and master the secrets of nature will assemble together at one spot to consider how best the tremendous new discoveries can be used for the benefit of mankind. Their meeting will constitute, in effect, a sort of international brains trust for human progress. Even from a statistical point of view, the conference is of an unprecedented character. We will see what will come of it.

Maybe Friday night or Saturday night we will ask Violet Dobbs or her daughter Jean to babysit the children and Oliver will take me to see the movie "To Catch a Thief" with Cary Grant and Grace Kelly or "Love is a Many-Splendored Thing" with William Holden and Jennifer Jones.

There is a knock on the door, a neighbour come to call? I turn the stove off in case it is a long visit—I always enjoy a neighbour's visit to break up the day—often long days with Oliver working in Hamilton—sometimes he doesn't get home. Many times he has been working too far away to come home except on the weekends. James had his sixth birthday on July 29th—quite a special young man, ready for school in September. Barbara will be four in September—what a beautiful head of curls—I love to make ringlets by wrapping the curls around my finger. Donald is very active, always hates to be confined to a playpen, always wants to roam; he was two in March. Shirley was one year old in June—she is a shy little one. Next month I will have a fifth child to look after.

It's a policeman at the door. Wonder what he wants?

"Your husband has been killed in an accident," he sadly tells me.

That doesn't make sense—what could he mean? I must be dreaming. He asked me to come to Hamilton to identify the body. I found a neighbour to watch the children and went with him. Oliver was 28 years old. He was working as a steel rigger on the construction of the 2,500,000 gallon Hamilton water tank on Fennell Avenue and 17th Street East. He plunged 50 feet to his death in the central tube—he slipped while he was bolting steel plates. He was wearing a safety belt at the time of the mishap, but where he was working it was impossible to fasten it to anything. Hamilton police reported that Oliver died immediately of multiple fractures after his fall at noon on August 8, 1955.

Mountain residents may have an extra million and a quarter gallons of water to use in three weeks time. James Stodart, waterworks design engineer for the city, reports the new tank at Fennel Avenue and East Seventeenth Street should be filled by that time. In early June the water shortage on the Mountain was seen once again when taps ran dry. So much water was used by residents, thirsty and concerned about parched lawns, that the existing three-quarter million gallon tank was drained on one occasion.

Steel work on the new tank was almost completed by August 13, and the painting was to start the next week. Mountain residents, short of water for several summers, raised a storm of protest when it was discovered the new tank would not be ready for use until at least the end of August. Could it happen that contractors on city work are pushed to the wall to fill their contracts by a definite date? The loss of a father to children will be felt through all their lives. The life of the wife will never be the same again either.

Everything is a blur, I feel like I am in a dream. Soon I will wake up and everything will be back to normal.

How will I manage? I live far from the city of Guelph, with only the passenger train service to get me in to town for major shopping. What can I do? I tried for months to find a place to rent in Guelph—but who wanted to have a family with four children to live in their home? Prospective landlords would say to themselves, think of the damage four—or five, because it looks like another is on the way—children could do! When I had three children, with the help of Dad, I was able to rent for awhile. But then along came number four.

I was a Mother with five children ages six and under—coins of gold—to raise on my own. How would I do it? Moffat was a little place, with a corner store, a post office, a school, some homes and farms.

Since I already took the train into Guelph on a regular basis to do my major shopping, I decided to look for a place to buy. With the money from an insurance policy, I had enough money for a down payment for a modest home. After much searching, I found a place on Old York Road, on the outskirts of Guelph, off Highway #7, across the road from the Ontario Reformatory grounds.

I could always see one step ahead, but didn't know how the years ahead would unfold. I was content to take one step at a time and follow my Master's leading.

Chapter 15

My Eldest Son

The following is a story written by Ida Donalda (Parker/Cromwell) Klughart about her oldest son, Oliver Lloyd Cromwell, followed by a poem Donalda wrote about Longwood, a place where they lived.

He was a happy lad with golden coloured hair; it changed very little, may have lost some of its shine. We lived at Killean, Ontario. He was born at Sheffield, Ontario, January 7, 1927. We (Ida Bell Donalda Parker and Archibald Samuel Cromwell) named him Oliver Lloyd. The Doctor had a problem getting him to cry. After trying several things, he put him in warm water, then held him out the door—that got results, it was forty below. In a week and a half we took him home; his bassinette was a small clothes basket, fitted with mattress and small pillow, nicely decorated. He slept in that till he got too long for it. His Dad said there was no money for a crib. He slept with us for awhile, but it was too crowded. I had a large wooden packing box and a pair of my brother's roller skates. I took the skates apart, placed the wheels on the bottom so the box would roll where I wanted it to. I had two large pillows my Mother (Martha Ann Stevenson Parker) had given me; I put them in the bottom, made a small mattress from a quilt batt I had, and put it on top of the pillows. It fit nicely under the window so Oliver didn't get a draft. I used to take him out in a sleigh someone loaned me.

At Easter a relative came; their son had the measles—Oliver and I both took the measles. It took six weeks or more to get over them. It was a busy summer; we had one cow and a few hens. When the weather turned cold,

Oliver's Dad got a self-feeder heater—we didn't have to keep putting coal in it. What we didn't know was that it had a crack in it. I wakened in the morning and I was real sick, so was my husband. Oliver seemed all right at first. We could smell the gas from the coal and opened all the windows and doors. We could have all died. I gave Oliver some breakfast—he heaved it up right away. It took two days before we were feeling all right. We got a different stove in a hurry.

Oliver was walking at ten months. He was also talking some, but didn't speak in sentences for awhile. We went to my folks (John and Martha Ann Parker) for Christmas; Oliver was given quite a few presents which he enjoyed very much. By March twelfth 1928 another boy (Donald Archie) had arrived. Oliver liked him and was a big help in keeping him quiet. The extra butter I made that we didn't need for our table, I sold for twenty-five cents a pound; I also sold eggs for fifteen cents a dozen. With the money I made, I was able to buy a second-hand baby buggy. We lived in Kirkwall for awhile, then moved to Galt. I was thankful for the baby buggy as we were on the outskirts of town. On April 25, 1929 a sister (Lena June) arrived. We had to cross the highway to go down town. Oliver would hang on to the buggy till there was no car in sight before he let us cross.

My Mother-in-law (Elizabeth Carter Cromwell) lived in Galt; her youngest daughter Lil was home for awhile. One afternoon about four o'clock Lil came to see if Oliver could come to their place for supper. I asked him if he would like to go with her for supper. He said he would go. A short time later they were back. Lil said he took his coat off, looked all around—she didn't think he missed anything. Then he got his coat and put it on and said he was going home. I don't think we ever did find out why he wouldn't stay.

In October we moved to a duplex on Water Street in Guelph. We had a small garden there, but there was no fence around the place. It started getting cold. I went to a sale one day and bought a large boys sleigh for fifty cents. There was a wooden bedstead in the basement. I asked my husband if he would make a frame out of it for the sleigh; he did. It looked like a small cutter; he put a seat in front for Oliver. Don and June lay down in it—Don wasn't walking yet. My mother gave me her old fur coat; I took the good part and made a robe to cover Oliver's knees; I had a blanket and quilt to cover the others. I took them out once. When I came back, I told my husband a rope was no good to pull it with; I asked him to put a tongue on it so that I would have some control over it. It worked fine then; we went many places with the sleigh. A friend came to visit me; she said she could smell gas—for some reason I couldn't smell it. I phoned the gas company; someone came and looked at it—they found a hole in the hose leading to the stove. I was thankful for the lady telling me she could smell gas.

There was a place for a small garden but there was no fence around it. When it came time to put the garden in, I took the children outside where I could watch them while I put the garden in. My house work was done in the afternoon while they rested. When it came time for the flowers, some Ladies from the terrace next to us said, "You'll never grow flowers there." I said, "Why not?" "We haven't had any flowers here since the Greek family moved in down the street. They had a restaurant downtown and the boys were often left home alone. It wasn't long till one boy came to see what I was doing. I told him I was getting the ground ready for flowers; I asked him if he would like to help plant the seeds. He said he would but he had never done it before. I showed him how to drop the seeds in—there were Morning Glories, Lily of the Valley, and Petunias. The two boys played with Oliver sometimes which helped a lot. I told them it would be a few weeks before we would see the flowers coming. The boys were nine and twelve. They came over about every other day; they thanked me for letting them help. Everyone had flowers that year.

Some people we knew bought some land about three miles north of the centre of town, on the Bedford Road. They sold my husband two acres in 1931; they built a shack for us to live in till we got a house built. It was June 1932 when we moved in. We had a garden there. Oliver was a big help in looking after the others—by this time there was another girl (Doris Mae born May 14, 1932). When Oliver was seven, I started him in school in the spring (1934). He seemed so lonesome I let Don start too. They got along well together. They went to school at Marden—they had a mile and a half to walk. In the fall, Archibald said he had rented the house to make some money. He rented a farm, hired his youngest brother (Herb Cromwell) to help—we had a bigger house and the school was a little closer. When Archibald decided to give up the farm, we couldn't get in our own house as it was still being rented. He rented a house on the outskirts of Guelph. The boys went to school in Guelph. In about a year and a half, we moved back in our own place. In the spring my husband was transferred to Hamilton with the railroad. He used to come home about every other weekend and bring some groceries and leave a little bit of money for milk and bread. One Saturday he didn't come; on Sunday we went to church with friends and had lunch with them afterwards. Oliver came and told me he saw his Dad go up to the house. We left our friends house and headed home. Archie said he left some bread and money on the table—there was one loaf of bread and twenty-five cents. I sought some advice—the result was money was left at the grocery store, money for milk was left at a farmer's—Oliver had to walk three quarters of a mile to get the milk. I still had a place for a garden. The river was close to our place and sometimes the children would go and watch the skaters. When spring arrived I dug up the garden, had quite a bit of it planted. Someone came to see how much I wanted for the oil drum sitting in the yard. I had no idea what they were worth, but I told him if he would plough the place for my potatoes he could have it. As he ploughed, I dropped the potatoes in behind him. He was kind enough to run the harrows over them to cover them—they were the best potatoes that year.

In the fall of 1936 we moved to Hamilton. My brother-in-law Charlie took us down. I was told the big bed would have to stay in the dining room—it wouldn't go upstairs because the stairs had a turn in them. During the next week Oliver and I put the bed upstairs. We made nice friends there. Oliver, Don and June were going to school. We lived on the shortest street in Hamilton, one block long, Margaret Street. In 1937 the Bailiff came and said our rent wasn't paid. We had to move out by the end of July. I applied for some welfare and the children and I went to stay with a relative. In September we moved to Longwood. Oliver was a big help there. They had two miles to go to school. (The poem on "Longwood" will explain what it was like there.)

The next move was to Drumbo. The boys cleaned the ice in the hockey rink. Eventually I got work in Drumbo. Oliver was a good cook. The children took their lunch to school; Oliver often had supper ready when I got home. When World War II started, those in the entrance class could get their entrance if they went to work on the farm. Just before Easter my sister Jean and her husband Harlan Wilson came to see if Oliver would go and work for them. I asked him if he would go and he said he would try it. They took him for a week. When they brought him back the next weekend they said they liked him fine. I think they were expecting to take him back with them—my sister asked if he could go back with them. I asked him, Oliver said no, he didn't want to go—they were disappointed. I was not going to force him if he did not want to go. Soon afterwards he got a job on a farm closer to home. He worked there that summer and the next. When he finished on the farm, he got a job in the furniture factory; he liked the job fine, but being inside he seemed to get sick at his stomach—not sure what caused it. Someone told me about a factory job doing war work—it paid a lot more money. I went to Guelph, got the job and got a place for my eldest daughter and I to stay. Don had a job on a farm. Oliver came home for awhile; he got a job in a foundry but the work was really heavy. He went to Hamilton and worked with a friend doing painting—on the inside and outside of houses. He painted our kitchen. Next he was working in steel as a steel rigger; then there was a steel strike and they couldn't get the steel so Oliver came home for awhile. Carl Saillian heard about him being home and phoned me to see if Oliver would come and dig out some of their basement—it had never been finished when the house was built. Oliver was a hard worker—the Saillians were so pleased that their basement was finished. They said they only knew of one other person who worked like him and he was a grown man. Oliver wouldn't be 18 till January—this was September or October.

Oliver went back to Hamilton working with steel. He was five feet eleven and a half inches tall. When he came home one weekend, he met my boarder, May Todd. They started dating and were married on February 26, 1949 in Guelph. Their first son James was born there, then Oliver's job took him to Fort Garry, Manitoba. In 1950 there was a flood with the Red River overflowing. They lived upstairs, but the water got too high for them to stay there. Around two thirty in the morning, James and his Mother were taken up the Pembina Highway in a boat to Fort Garry and later to Winnipeg. Later they were told that if they had relatives they could go to, their way would be paid—the men were kept at the university to help with the cattle. May went east and stayed with her cousin Rosa Saillian and family. May gave birth to twins while in Guelph; they were premature, one lived a day (Linda) and the other (Louise) lived a week. May wasn't eager to go back out west, but Oliver told her he was going to let his beard grow till she came back.

In 1951 two doctors told me I needed a change. I decided to visit Oliver where they were living in Winnipeg. I came by bus and Oliver was at the bus depot to meet me. He had a small truck and lifted my trunk into it. He told me he would help me find my oldest brother, Elmer, whom I hadn't seen for about thirty years. He was able to get quite a bit of information before we left. We got to Lac du Bonnet, phoned the people he stayed with, they said he was working in Pine Falls. We stayed the night in Lac Du Bonnet and left the next morning. We came to a sign pointing to the left which said Pine

Falls—to the right we would go to the place where my brother stayed. Oliver said, "Mom, if you don't mind I think we'll go this way first." It was a good thing we did; we met my brother and the fellow he stayed with coming to find us. We went back to their place, had a good visit with my brother. Oliver and Elmer went out and picked an eleven quart basket of blueberries which we took back with us. That was Labour Day weekend and it was getting late when we got back to Winnipeg. Oliver's work took him to Moose Jaw. Don was with the oil drillers—the oil well was at Avonlea and Don and his wife Lil were living in Milestone. Oliver asked if I would come to Moose Jaw and look for a place for them to live. I went there and walked over most of Moose Jaw—no one wanted children. There didn't seem to be any boarding places there. Finally Oliver brought his wife and two children (James and Barbara) to Milestone. They had their own room, but ate with Don and Lil. After several months, he was able to get a place to live at Boharm, west of Moose Jaw, on #1 highway. Next they wanted to transfer him to British Columbia. His wife didn't want to go any further west, so they went east. (Was May missing her family? Her father was living in Guelph and so was her cousin Rosa.) They were in Sarnia for a year or so and their son Donald was born there. Next they moved to Guelph—same thing there—no children wanted. May and the children went to stay with her cousin Rosa; they stored their furniture in May's father (William Todd)'s garage. Oliver's work took him many places, Whitby for one, Quebec, New Brunswick. Then his work took him to Hamilton. They were able to get a house to live in, in Moffat. Oliver had twenty miles to drive to work. The dampness had taken the veneer off the furniture (while it was in storage); Oliver was restoring the last piece. He was killed at his work building the water tower on the west mountain of Hamilton. He was wearing his safety belt but there was no place to fasten it. I lived in Regina at the time, but as soon as the telegram came I made arrangements to go. First the doctor wanted to see me—he explained how badly Oliver was hurt, but also said that his death was instant. An elderly lady asked her daughter and son-in-law to be sure and tell me how much they appreciated Oliver—he used to help her husband with various things. After her husband retired, Oliver used to go and talk with him and help him; retirement was hard for him to accept. After her husband passed away, Oliver would go and see what he could do for her—it was so much appreciated. One person said Oliver just finished a picket fence for them—they didn't have a clue how to build one. Another person said Oliver put Congo wall in their bathroom and kitchen—it was something new, they didn't know how.

Letters kept coming in with money, because we knew Oliver. His wife went to the grocery store—when she went to pay the bill, the storekeeper said he was given money to pay for the groceries—the answer was always the same, because we knew Oliver. The Senior men put on a ball game that brought in some money for the family. The day of the funeral a man in his eighties walked around the casket and said why couldn't it have been me instead of that nice young fellow. So many came to me to tell me of his good deeds. He was always good to me. I.D.K.

Longwood

Now Longwood is a great old place
The place where I abide,
You'll find us down by the railroad
On the cold north side.

This section house is sitting here
You'll find it all alone,
And now I must tell you about the place
That I must call my home.

There's a creek that runs behind the house
They say it overflows,
There isn't much water in it now,
I don't know where it goes.

There is a house across the road, there
Are bachelors in it now
There are no more neighbours, very close
It's a lonesome place, I vow.

The school's two miles away from here,
For it's down by the store,
There were eight children going to school,
And now there are two more.

This Longwood is a funny place,
But pretty in the fall,
The store is where they always say
We'll have it next time you call.

There are miles and miles of endless track
That's running east and west,
It got its name from all the trees
They are what I love the best.

They are being cleared out all the time,
The woods will soon be gone,
Six men are sawing at the trees,
And now it won't be long.

For when I'm just outside my door,
The noise is ringing far,
They bring the trees a crashing down,
The lovely woods to mar.

They are scaring all the squirrels away,
The birds have left my door,
I cannot like this Longwood now,
I might have once before.

There are beechnuts and the oaks and maples,
I wonder where they'll go?
But it's making work for lots of men
Then we must have it so.

It's four miles into Melbourne here,
And six to Caradoc,
It's four miles down to Appin, too
The railroad's built on rock.

It's nine miles straight to Strathroy
On the road past our abode,
It's about ten miles to Glencoe here,
On a mighty rough built road.

Now London is the nearest city,
The miles are twenty-three,
Why they built this house in such a place,
Seems very queer to me.

Now Longwood is a lovely place
To see it in the fall,
When the trees are all in colours dressed,
You'll like it best of all.

There are lots of walnuts, beechnuts,
And hickory nuts this year,
And anyone that loves the trees,
Would like to see it here.

                        Ida Donalda Klughart—1937

Chapter 16

Go Over, Go Under, Go Around, Or Go Through, But Never Give Up

I attended St. George's Sunday School, connected with Anglican Christ Church. The Sunday School was held in a building not far from our home. The Church, to which we went a few times a year, was across the Moira River. Sometimes we took a bus uptown to the foot bridge and then walked over to the Church at the corner of Catherine and Coleman Streets.

The first year of attending Sunday School, I missed out on completing perfect attendance, because of being involved in an accident. My brother was taking me to a department store on Thursday, December 1st, 1927 when I was hit by a car and received a deep cut at the base of my left ear. After remaining overnight in hospital, I came home but had to take it easy for a few days. Consequently I was not able to attend Sunday School that week and could not receive my year's pin. I was very disappointed. My brother accompanied me to the store. It must have been quite a shock for him to see me hit by the car and be unconscious. Someone brought him home and came in to tell Mom the news. When I returned to public school, I wore a tam to hold the bandage in place.

"Girl Struck by Car on Front Street—Little May Todd suffers head injuries which are not serious—driver not blamed. May Todd, the seven year old daughter of Mr. and Mrs. William Todd, 350 Bleecker Avenue, suffered head injuries when she was thrown to the pavement in front of the Canadian Department Store on Front Street by a passing motor car about five o'clock yesterday afternoon. Mr. Fred Rawson, driver of the car, was absolved of all blame by the police. According to eye witnesses the little girl who was on her way to see Santa Claus at the Canadian Department Store, started from the east side of Front Street and, not noticing the Rawson car, ran directly into the side of it. She was knocked down with some force and was unconscious when picked up.

Mr. Rawson immediately stopped his car and picking up the little girl rushed her to the hospital where her injuries were treated by Dr. G. H. Stoble. A deep cut at the base of the left ear is the chief injury and, while she will be confined to her home for some time, no serious results are likely to follow. She was taken from the hospital to her home this morning . . ." (Belleville paper)

I completed my first year of perfect attendance in 1928; the second in 1929; the third in December 1931, and the first term of my fourth year in June 1932.

Our Sunday School had adopted "Little's Cross and Crown System" for increasing attendance. Each pupil was given a celluloid pin to start with. For the first term of three months (13 Sundays) attendance without absence I earned the No. 1 bronze pin; for the second the No. 2 gun metal finish; for the third the No. 3 silver plated; for the fourth the No. 6 Solid gold pin. The gold pin was presented with a handsome lithographed certificate with seal and ribbon attached. Each of the other pins was returned when the next higher grade was received.

Pupils absent without excuse lose the part of the term already made but may begin a new term the next Sunday they attend. Pupils attending an additional year after the four terms earn the hand engraved wreath to encircle the No. 6 pin; following this, the third, fourth and fifth year bars, comprising when complete the handsome solid gold jewel. As the Cross and Crown pin was the official badge of the School, every pupil was encouraged to strive to earn the No. 6 solid gold one as soon as possible.

For each additional year another seal and ribbon is added to the certificate. The solid gold star and cross pendants, containing genuine birth stones were given as rewards to pupils who attend church services. These were to be attached to the No. 6 solid gold pin or to the wreath and year bars. The birth stones for each month are as follows:

January	Garnet	July	Ruby
February	Amethyst	August	Sardonyx
March	Bloodstone	September	Sapphire
April	Diamond	October	Opal
May	Emerald	November	Topaz
June	Pearl or Agate	December	Turquoise

After moving to Malvern, then England, and back to Canada, we attended various churches that were in our neighbourhoods.

I was raised in the Anglican Church, but in Guelph after we moved to Old York Road, we attended the nearby Baptist Church on York Road within easy walking distance from our home. The children went to Sunday School, we all attended church services, when young the children went to Happy Hour which I helped out with, and later the girls went to Pioneer Girls Club, and the boys went to Christian Service Brigade.

In 1964 I came in contact with the Plain Truth magazine through my cousin Rosa. It was published by the Worldwide Church of God. I began receiving the Plain Truth regularly in January 1965, which introduced me to many booklets, articles, and the Ambassador College Bible Correspondence Course through which I learned many new things I had not known before. It was a very exciting course and as I dug deeper into the Bible, I saw where God had commanded His people to keep annual holy days. We began attending the Church of God in Toronto on April 16, 1966, just after the spring feasts of Passover and Days of Unleavened Bread. The Feasts of the Lord, as they are called in Leviticus 23, picture God's great plan of salvation for mankind. As we keep these, in their seasons, we can rejoice in knowing that God will bring to pass His great plan.

We kept the Feast of Pentecost and Trumpets in Toronto, and the Day of Atonement at Leisureland in Hamburg, New York. Mr. Antion was minister of two churches, one in Buffalo, New York, U.S.A., and the other in Toronto, Ontario, Canada. The two groups combined on holy days, and services might be either in Toronto or Buffalo.

My family and I attended our first Feast of Tabernacles, in Mount Pocono, Pennsylvania, in the fall of 1967. This was the farthest point away from home that my children had ever been. The six of us stayed in one large room in Grand View Tower at Mount Airy Lodge. The Church had erected a huge tent where services were held each day to teach us God's way of life.

When it rained, the rain poured in through the roof around all the tent poles, with people opening their umbrellas inside to try to stay dry—quite an experience. The children had an opportunity to go horseback riding and to take the ski-lift up Camelback Mountain.

In 1968 we were able to transfer to the local church in Kitchener. That fall we were again in the Poconos with four children and I staying at Naomi Cottages, Cresco, Pennsylvania. By this time Jim was living on his own in Toronto, so he went to the feast with some other fellows in the church and stayed at Mo-Nom-o-Nock Inn. The tent was gone and a new tabernacle building had been constructed that would seat 16,000 people for services, making for a much more pleasant environment, also being warmer during the very cool fall weather in the mountains.

For twenty years, I had the opportunity to travel to various sites throughout the United States and Canada to celebrate the Feast of Tabernacles. It was our annual vacation and we were able to see the sites nearby each location.

For my entire life, Bible reading and study was an important part of each day. Living the principles was the most important, and teaching them to my children, who in turn taught them to their children.

Chapter 17

Joy Everywhere

Griffin's Theatre was built on the corner of Church and East Bridge Streets, and was near the Armouries. Opera was projected to the local lovers of musical drama, and also anything else of musical interest. Travelling Minstrel Shows played there, as did "Uncle Tom's Cabin". Lively vaudeville acts spiced with the hit tunes of the day, Floradora girls prancing and dancing in gaudy costumes, itinerant jugglers and magicians with their stock in trade novelties, a noted singer or instrumentalist stopping off for an evening of culture while enroute to larger centres, military groups, and local talent were what made Griffin's Opera House a centre of activity for Belleville and the surrounding area. Silent movies were played in the early 1900s, with the Talkies of the late 1920s quickly shifting the scene from live performances to those "in the can".

Sometimes Mom kept me home from school and took me with her to see a movie. One was called, "Uncle Tom's Cabin", and it was sad. My mother cried!

There were two movie houses in Belleville, the Griffin Theatre and the Capitol Theatre. Another movie in 1928, was about the First World War. "Wings" with Clara Bow and Charles "Buddy" Rodgers was also playing at one theatre. Willie and I went to Saturday morning matinee at the Griffin Theatre. I liked the action movies with cowboys and Indians, and also the serials that were continued each week. They were very exciting and we could hardly wait a week to see how things turned out.

Albert, Merton and Morley Plunkett, three brothers with good voices, brought fame to Orillia, their birthplace. During World War I, they volunteered to produce entertainment to boost the morale of the war-weary troops. They took the name The Dumbells from the insignia of the 3rd Division, two crossed dumbbells and the name became widely known in the trenches, in London, across Canada and even on Broadway.

Their early shows consisted of comedy sketches, songs and dance numbers performed by the amateur soldier-singers. From the outset they knew that to win their audience, who had been living in tough battlefield conditions for months, they would have to keep the fare light and happy, so the music they chose was a mix of popular ballads, hits and comic songs. The soldier audience did not look forward to the first show, and at first actually threw things at the stage. But female impersonator Ross Hamilton ("Marjorie") gave them their first glimpse of a lady—even though not a real one—in months, singing "Hello My Dearie" in a falsetto soprano voice, and quickly won them over. Al Plunkett, costumed in top hat and silk tailcoat, was also successful with his rendition of the popular American song, "Those Wild, Wild Women Are Making a Wild Man of Me."

They wrote humorous skits on everyday events in the soldiers' lives, poking fun at military discipline and the hardships of trench warfare. The orderly room, sick parade, muddy trenches, and the Commanding Officer's headquarters—no subject was immune from the Dumbell's saucy interpretation. Among their popular repertoire were First World War hit songs such as "Mademoiselle from Armentieres," "Pack Up Your Troubles in Your Old Kit Bag" and "It's a Long Way to Tipperary." The Dumbells also performed Canadian patriotic songs such as "It's Canada (The Land For Me)". Jack Ayre, their regular pianist composed the group's theme song, "The Dumbell Rag." Often Canadian soldiers would whistle this tune while marching from the performance to the front lines. The all-soldier review was a resounding success, staging shows in the trenches and later in peacetime. The Dumbells' motto was "Any place, Anywhere" and the troupe often performed on makeshift stages with the sounds of the front in the background. The Dumbells performed wherever the Canadian troops were fighting, constantly on the move across France. Among the properties and equipment they transported with them was their battered upright piano which several strong soldiers would be assigned to tote on to the stage. During one show a German shell crossed the stage in mid-performance; fortunately, it did no damage. Peacetime shows continued from 1919 to 1932, and patrons of the Orillia Opera House always gave them an enthusiastic reception when they played there. They even did a stint on Broadway in 1921. In 1939, Mert Plunkett became the overseas entertainment supervisor for the Canadian Legions Auxiliary services. His composition "We're On Our Way" was sung by soldiers en route to Europe and became popular in England.

Vera Lyn and Ann Shelton were two top singers during World War II. Vera Lynn, just three years older than me, was the voice of encouragement for the troops and the British people. "We'll Meet Again" and "The White Cliffs of Dover" were two of her many popular songs. In 1940, having been singing since age seven when she sang in a working men's club, she began her own radio series, "Sincerely Yours," sending messages to British troops stationed abroad. She visited new mothers in hospitals and sent messages to their husbands overseas. She gave outdoor concerts for soldiers in Egypt, India and Burma. The nostalgic lyrics to "We'll Meet Again" ("We'll meet again, don't know where, don't know when, but I know we'll meet again some sunny day") had a great appeal to the many people separated from loved ones during the war.

Lena Horne, an American singer and actress, the same age as Vera Lynn, both being born in 1917, sang in night clubs and performed in movies, such as "Stormy Weather" and "Cabin in the Sky."

Ann Shelton, born in 1923, was a popular English singer who provided inspirational songs for soldiers on radio broadcasts and in person at military bases during World War II. Ann sang duets with Bing Crosby in "Easter Parade" and "I'll Get By."

"In the Mood" by Glen Miller was another popular tune. Glen's plane crashed as he was on his way to entertain troops in France. I liked the song, "As Time Goes By" from the film "Casablanca", with Humphrey Bogart and Ingrid Bergman. Abbot and Costello films kept us laughing through the war with their comedy routines. "Who's on First" was on the radio in 1938. Abbott was the devious straight man and Costello was the stumbling, dimwitted laugh-getter. They made thirty-six films together between 1940 and 1956. Abbott and Costello were among the most popular and highest-paid entertainers in the world during World War II. I saw a lot of pictures over those years, going to shows at least twice a week and sometimes again at the weekend.

From the late 1930s to the early 1950s, the original Ink Spots were a popular and influential singing group. They were an African American vocal quartette who helped define the musical genre that led to rhythm and blues and rock and roll. The original group, of Ivory "Deek" Watson (Second Tenor, guitar), Jerry Daniels (Lead Tenor, guitar, ukulele), Charlie Fuqua (Baritone, guitar, ukelele) and Orville "Hoppy" Jones (bass, cello—strung as a bass and not played with a bow but picked and slapped like a double bass, string bass) started out singing fast "jump" tunes in 1934 and their early recordings reflected this style. The group became famous after the arrival of Bill Kenny in early 1936, and the group's addition of a ballad style featuring Bill Kenny's high tenor and Hoppy's "talking" chorus. Their most famous recording was "If I Didn't Care", with some of their other hits being "You Wonderful Thing", "Back in Nagasaki", "Swingin' On the Strings", "Your Feet's Too Big". "I Don't Want Sympathy, I Want Love" reached #1 on the pop music charts and was listed for nine weeks in 1939.

The early experiences of my life and the teachers who taught me at school imparted to me a lifelong love of learning. One of my favourite subjects was history. Studying cause and effect and how and why man continues to excel in acquiring knowledge and accomplishing great technological wonders and yet keeps on repeating major mistakes can clearly be recognized and understood by even a casual student of history. My second most enjoyable class was geography, being informed about the different peoples, cultures, countries, and natural beauties of the world, and the positive impact of many offset by the negative. Throughout my life these things were a joy for me to behold.

Beginning when I was young, Mom instilled in me a deep affection for the parallel world of the movies. I was fascinated and drawn into this place where writers, directors, actors and actresses would present visual stories with facial expression, body language, and inflection of voice and the whole gamut of human emotions. I marveled at how the best actors became whichever character they were portraying. There were innate attributes within them: dynamic personality, "it" factor, "star" quality, key-light which made them educational, enlightening and entertaining over and over again.

The movies which emphasized people, the human condition and the incredible potential for either good or evil, great accomplishments or tremendous failures, over events, situations and circumstances, were the most appealing. For me, the genres of movies which best represented and reflected my hunger for discovering important lessons of history and the peoples of the world were War films and Romances. Because of the enormous effect World War I and World War II had on my life, films of this period held a special attraction, interest, fondness and meaning for me.

Negative and destructive personality and character traits in a 'leader', or a person in authority, could have a similar effect on the situation and course of history. A true leader would inspire and motivate his men to accomplish the 'impossible'. The difficult we do immediately, the impossible takes a little longer.

Other types of films such as comedies, dramas, musicals and westerns also gave me great pleasure and much pondering and reflecting later. Just as the success of a battle depends upon preparation, training, leadership, cooperation and teamwork, inspired plans and ideas, adaptability and adjustments and an element of good luck, a great movie requires the same. The gelling and coming together of all those in front of the camera must be in harmony with the team behind the lens and with the props, costumes and set decorations.

Another requisite is the music score and songs to set the pace, the mood by drawing out the appropriate emotions, and transfer the story smoothly from scene to scene. I was able to recognize pieces of music and songs and this aided me in obtaining the greatest enjoyment, understanding, appreciation and benefit possible from each movie. I was always humming and singing along, making watching a movie a most enjoyable experience—for myself, as well as for anyone watching with me. I often shared humorous comments over a cup of tea after watching a movie with one of my children.

I preferred a strong male actor to drive a good story. However, the second and third lead, the lead actress and appropriate character actors, all with charm, charisma, appeal and screen presence, were required. The lead actor, even with great talent, training and star presence could not stand alone.

If I made a list of a thousand movies, I still might miss some of my favourites. Many of these films I watched over and over again. Some, I had to rely upon the memories from my childhood when I went on a weekly basis with my mother to the pictures. Others I have watched on television throughout my lifetime, sometimes once or twice, and if I was more fortunate, numerous times. Even experiencing a picture just once, had a tremendous impact on me.

Some of my favourite lead actors were Humphrey Bogart, Marlon Brando, Clark Gable, Cary Grant, Charlton Heston, William Holden, Rock Hudson, Burt Lancaster, Steve McQueen, Paul Newman, Gregory Peck, Sidney Poitier, James Stewart, Spencer Tracy and John Wayne. Other lead, second and third lead and character actors that I enjoyed, among a long list, were Yul Brynner, Kirk Douglas, Henry Fonda, George Peppard, Robert Redford, Frank Sinatra.

Lead actresses that provided enjoyment to me were Lauren Bacall, Ingrid Bergman, Joan Crawford, Betty Davis, Greta Garbo, Audrey Hepburn and Grace Kelly.

Just a few of my favourite films from World War I are: The African Queen, All Quiet on the Western Front, Anne of Green Gables: The Continuing Story, The Dawn Patrol, A Farewell to Arms, The White Cliffs of Dover, Wings.

Favourite films from World War II included: Attack!, The Bridge on the River Kwai, Casablanca, The Desert Fox, The Great Escape, The Guns of Navarone, The Longest Day, PT 109, The Purple Heart, Run Silent Run Deep, To the Shores of Tripoli.

Favourite films with a post-war setting were All My Sons, The Best Years of Our Lives, Exodus, Lilies of the Field, On the Beach.

Great love stories enjoyed many, many times included All That Heaven Allows, An Affair to Remember, The Enchanted Cottage, First Love, Love Is a Many-Splendored Thing, Penny Serenade. And just a very small selection of other great romantic films that I have enjoyed are Adam's Rib, Breakfast at Tiffany's, Christmas in Connecticut, For Love of Ivy, Gone With the Wind, Jane Eyre, The Long Hot Summer, Message in a Bottle, Roman Holiday, Sayonara, Send Me No Flowers, Three Coins in the Fountain, Wuthering Heights.

Chapter 18

Second Chance at Love

Happiness is a journey, not a destination. So work like you don't need money, love like you've never been hurt, and, dance like no one's watching.

In 1968 I met Orlin Stewart when we attended services in Kitchener. We began dating at that time, although he lived miles away, on Highway #3 east of Dunnville, in the Niagara Peninsula. Orlin's wife had died a year earlier. He had two sons, Rodney and Cleason.

In the fall the children and I were in the Poconos. Orlin travelled there in his father's car with Cleason. We spent much time together at The Feast.

Sometimes Orlin would travel from Dunnville to Guelph mid-week to pick us up and take us to Bible Study in Kitchener. Often he brought a box of bananas and other food with him. In the winter the boys shoveled snow from the driveway so Orlin would be able to park his car.

Orlin and I became engaged on January 15, 1969, and were married on March 16 at the home of our minister, Mr. Gary Antion, in Toronto. We honeymooned in Niagara Falls and stayed at Cliffside Motel.

This is a poem that Orlin wrote when we were married and our two families became one.

S.C. Number Nine

We'll sail this ship away,
We'll do what God commands,
And then we'll understand,
When we reach the promised land.

We'll sail this ship with joy,
Though Satan would destroy,
With love so tender sweet,
Our cargo we will keep.

We'll sail this ship with might,
With God our guiding light,
With Satan we'll compete,
We'll kneel at Jesus' feet.

We'll sail upon the blue,
The captain and his crew,
And we will not be late,
God gave us our first mate.

We'll sail this ship, so fine,
May God say that you're mine,
And we will tow the line,
On S.C. number nine.

And now we've left the shore
We've got our trials galore
But we will overcome
Until the job is done.

We had already decided to sell the home in Guelph and move to Dunnville, which we did at the end of April. Until an addition was made on Orlin's home, Barbara and Shirley slept over at Grandma Stewart's house which was in front of ours, nearer the highway.

During the spring and summer of 1969, a two-storey addition with three rooms on each floor was added. Orlin did all the work, building, plumbing, electrical work, with the help of Don and Bill. The boys were able to put into practice the things they were learning at school, it being a good experience for them. Now they each had their own bedroom upstairs, and the girls shared a room downstairs. A small bathroom was made for the girls and me, and a shower put in upstairs for the boys.

Orlin and I now had six teenagers in the family, which made a lot of washing each week. Before the new part was built, I felt like a pioneer. There was no room for my washing machine, so the girls and I had to wash the clothes outside. With nearly three acres of property, the kids had lots of room to play. Gardening was a big project and everyone helped. There were chickens to look after and Orlin bought calves to fatten and sell. One time the door of the barn was left open and the calves got out. The family were running all over the place rounding them up.

It was a great place to raise a family and though there was always work to do, we had our enjoyable moments too. Orlin took the kids to Crystal Beach a few times and even went on the rides with them. I think my family were more happy now they had a father.

The beach area of Crystal Beach was a major attraction because of a gentle slope that ran for some distance underwater with no drop-offs or undertow. A pier was built and a ferry service was set up to bring people to the park. Amusement rides included a ferris wheel, and various roller coasters. The "Wild Mouse" ride started with a chain pull up the left side to the top which was about 12 to 15 metres off the ground. The cars then traversed a path back and forth across the top of the framework with 7 or 8 sharp 180 degree turns at the edges of the frame, all the while building speed. At the end of this course at the top, the track dropped within the framework to become a violent rage of a coaster with very quick drops. The merry-go-round had two chariots, twenty-three horses and twenty-one other animals including a camel, giraffe, lion, wolf, and a St. Bernard dog.

The most excitement was generated when we were preparing to go to the Pocono Mountains for the Feast of Tabernacles, our annual holiday. In 1970 we stayed in a mountain home. We visited the Memorytown Mt. Pocono General Store featuring old-fashioned candies, preserves, pickles, pretzels, rag rugs, hats, handbags, jugs, bottles, toys, soap, candies, and many other interesting items.

Three more poems Orlin wrote:

> I thought I'd write a poem
> To the kids that I call mine,
> Just a word to tell you
> I think that you're real fine.
>
> I'd like to just say thank you
> For a job you did so great,
> For the way you helped to sail the ship
> And for the one we call first mate.
>
> I'd like to say I need you
> To help me with this boat.
> It's going to take a lot of work
> To keep our ship afloat.
>
> I'd like to say I need you
> To pray for me each night
> That I might have the courage
> For the battles we'll have to fight.

Barbara Raué

I'd like to say I am happy
To have you for my crew.
I'd like to also tell you
I love our first mate too.

I am proud to be your Captain,
My life with you to share,
To prove to you I love you,
To prove I really care.

I am proud to call you sailors
Of the S.C. Number 9,
For now we know the meaning of
We will tow the line.

I want to be your Captain
And sail upon the blue.
Not just to be your Captain,
But to be your Father too.
(written 1969-70)

Poem to Shirley

This is our lovely Daughter
Her name is Shirley May
She is kind of shy and beautiful
And we sure love her that way.

We like to see her laughing
And then we see her dimples
We like to see her brilliant smile
It helps to hide her pimples.

We like to see her golden hair
We like to see her dancing
We like to see her girlish flair
We know she's near romancing.

We like to see her sparkling eyes
They seem to kind of glisten
Someday they'll surely please her Man
He'll stop and look and listen.

We know our Shirley's growing up
Her actions tell us so
We love her oh so very much
More than she'll ever know.
Mom & Dad (December 31, 1969)

Barbara Raué

      Dear Sailors,   March 16, 1970

It's just a year ago today
That I married our first mate
And I became your Captain
To sail our ship of light.

So thanks to all you sailors
For the job you've done so well
It's made my job more easy
In more ways than I can tell.

We can vision the world tomorrow
As we sail this sea of life
And we'll all pull together
For the first mate is my wife.

So sailors I salute you
On this our special day
I thank our God that made us
For sending you my way.
      With much love,
    Your Captain and first mate
     Mom and Daddy

During the years 1970-1976, Orlin and I made a few visits to Harley and Glady Sheir's cottage at Bay Lake near Novar and Huntsville. Glady was Orlin's sister.

Huntsville is a town in the Muskoka Region of Ontario with the area being settled in 1869 by Captain George Hunt, who built a small agricultural centre there. In 1870, a post office was built and the area was named Huntsville after Hunt, who was the first postmaster. In the following year, the Muskoka Colonization Road reached the area. A water route north from Port Sydney to Huntsville opened in 1877 and a railway route was built by the Northern and Pacific Junction Railway in 1885 which encouraged development. The community became an important industrial area in the late 19th century and had several saw, planing and shingle mills, as well as a tannery. Today, the many lakes and hills in the area, combined with the town's proximity to both Algonquin Park and Toronto, make Huntsville and the Muskoka region a major tourist destination.

On Tuesday, November 3, 1970, we arrived at Bay Lake in the early morning. The next day we went out on the float for a relaxing time on the water. Orlin planted a horse chestnut tree. On Friday he put ceiling tile on a bedroom. The week was over far too soon and we headed for home on Tuesday.

In July 1971, arriving in Bay Lake we found our tree alive and healthy. The next day the weather was beautiful, sunny and hot, near 80°F. In the morning we went for a ride in the rowboat using the oars to propel us along. In the afternoon I got right in the water to cool off. Orlin mowed the lawn and we shopped at Novar. Shopping in Huntsville helped us to learn patience as the town was full of cars. Orlin started putting strapping on Glady's bedroom ceiling and finished half of the tiles. The next day, after completing the ceiling, we had a lovely afternoon boat ride using the motor. Thrilling! We phoned the kids, had supper in Huntsville and went to a show. We had our last boat ride, water quite choppy, getting cooler. We left in beautiful sunshine and had clear skies all the way home.

On our trip in October 1972, Glady had us speaking and singing over the tape recorder. Orlin wanted some exercise with the oars, so we took the boat out on Sunday afternoon. On Tuesday we had a little bit of snow (October 24). On Thursday I had my hair shampooed and set in Huntsville. Orlin worked on the garage for the tractor. We enjoyed another ride in the motorboat. It was lovely on the lake. After that Orlin took me for a ride up the laneway on the tractor. I sat on the back, on the hydraulic lift bar. It was more of a thrill coming back down the hill! On the Sabbath we packed a lunch and went to Sudbury for church services, after which we ate our lunch along the way back to the cottage. We saw the old Dionne home and a new building they are putting up: a sign said something about the quints antique shop. On Sunday, October 29, we helped take the float out of the water and brought the small boat up. On Monday it was cold and sunny; Orlin got the garage door on. We piled new lumber in the garage, put the boat in, also the tractor. A nice day with much work accomplished. We packed our belongings in the car ready to go home the next morning. That night we watched the election results on television with Pierre Elliot Trudeau remaining in office as our Prime Minister. Unable to leave in the morning because of a migraine headache, we finally left at four p.m. Upon arriving home at eight, I went straight to bed.

In May 1973, we arrived in the rain to meet black flies. One day we went to Burk's Falls and brought home lumber for Harley. The area around Burk's Falls was first settled by loggers during the 1860s. The only route into the region at that time was up the Magnetawan River from Georgian Bay, or through the forests of the unsurveyed townships north of Bracebridge. After 1875, travellers came north from Muskoka by way of the Rosseau-Nipissing Colonization Road. A steamboat service was established to the foot of the falls from the village of Magnetawan and railway service came to Burk's Falls in 1886. The village was named after David Francis Burk of Oshawa, Ontario who named the location and the waterfall on the site after himself after he selected the land surrounding the waterfall in the Free Land Grant Act.

On our 1974 trip in May, I got sunburn on my arms and face, and especially my nose, as we were able to spend lots of time outdoors, and on the float on the water. Our chestnut tree was alive and healthy.

In October 1975, we drove to Bay Lake in our Chevrolet, a leisurely drive with a couple of stops along the way. On our shopping trip into Huntsville, Orlin bought me silver earrings. We spent the Sabbath quietly at the cottage. Uncle Orvy and Aunt Lil Foster were over for supper on Sunday; their beautiful cottage was next door to the Scheir's. Orvy took us out on the lake in the lovely boat that he had built. It was on pontoons and had a roof over top.

On July 18, 1976, we arrived at Bay Lake about 10:30 a.m. to surprise Harley and Glady. There were lots of boats on the lake and water skiers as well. Glady loaned me black shorts and a black blouse which I used for a bathing suit in order to enjoy the warm water of the lake. On Wednesday Glady cooked hotdogs outside over charcoal. The mosquitoes were bad. On Thursday there were clear skies, it was sunny and hot. Harley, Glady, Orlin and I, got the float into the water (that took a lot of work). We sat on the float for awhile and then ate supper outside again. On Friday it was sunny and hot! Hot! Hot! I sat on the float and dangled my feet in the water. Believe it or not, Orlin did too! By evening the weather was sultry. I got a terrific tan, best yet! Their son Doug, with Muriel and Tiffy, arrived about eleven p.m. Sunday there was fog rising off the lake, looked like the beginning of another lovely day. We left at seven a.m. and arrived home at twelve noon.

When he was full, one of Orlin's favourite sayings was, "I am suffancified." We always teased him saying that was not a word, but he insisted it was because he got it from one of his school teachers. Orlin got bananas quite cheaply from Elroy's store in Dunnville, so we ate them regularly. My kids loved the banana splits he made for them.

Don had been urging us to come out West, but Dad wasn't yet ready to fly! However, he surprised me one summer by suggesting that we go to the Feast in Calgary. I thought he was kidding but he was really serious. He felt that the boys needed to see us, so in 1979 we headed west. Bill went with us. We stayed in the Westward Inn. The boys were really glad to see us! They spent many an hour talking to us in our hotel room. We had quite a few meals together. Dad and I really enjoyed the delicious western steaks. We went to see a horse race with Jim while we were there. We had rented a car but Dad was not feeling up to driving very much, so Don took us to several places in the area. We had an enjoyable feast, and then went to Banff to stay with Don for a few days holiday. He had prepared a casserole of porcupine meatballs, potatoes, onions and tomatoes for us. It was very good!

Don worked for Southern Music Company of Calgary and was manager in Banff at the time, installing and repairing pool tables, juke boxes and arcade games. He had a pool table in his living room and he and Dad had enjoyable times playing pool. We went in the gondola up Sulphur Mountain, and made a trip to Lake Louise.

Over the years, changes were made in the house. Our former bedroom was turned into a living room. We had a lovely gas fireplace, and Orlin built the bookcase in the wall. He continued to work on the inside of the house and made a new bathroom. We bought panelling for the spare room upstairs and planned to have it for our bedroom. It was a lovely bright room with two windows for a nice cross breeze. However, Orlin was not well and couldn't stand the hammering at that time, even if Bill were to do it. He was in hospital a couple of times in Dunnville and then at McMaster Medical

Centre in Hamilton. The doctor wanted him to have by-pass surgery but he decided against it.

My brother, his wife Joan, and son John came over from England to visit us. I had not seen Willie for thirty-three years. Rosa and Carl brought them to our home in Dunnville.

On his birthday, May 18, 1981, Orlin collapsed on the floor and died before the ambulance arrived. He was 59 years of age. I arranged for him to be buried beside his first wife at Maple Lawn Cemetery, Wainfleet. My brother was able to attend the funeral. Soon after their return to England, his wife also died.

Bill and I put the paneling on the upstairs room and I bought the rug that Orlin and I had chosen, also new bedroom furniture. Finally I was able to use the nicest room in the house. When Don came home for a visit he put a new door on it.

Chapter 19

Travel

With Orlin gone, I made my own arrangements to be able to attend the feasts in the fall each year and to see some of the tourist sites.

In the fall of 1982, I visited Black Creek Pioneer Village which consists of thirty authentically restored buildings, furnished largely through the generous donations from public-spirited friends of the Village. Many of the priceless gifts in the homes have been treasured by families for over one hundred years. There is a grain barn, fire house, harness shop and saddlery, homes, post office, blacksmith shop, school, Roblin's Mill powered by a water wheel, church, boot and shoe shop, carriage works, cabinet maker's shop, printing office, doctor's home, weavers shop, broom maker's shop, slaughter house and a cider mill.

In 1986 Bill, Jane and I attended the Feast of Tabernacles in Penticton, British Columbia. We flew out to Vancouver but were not able to see that city because we had only a short time before catching a smaller plane to the Feast site. Penticton takes full advantage of its dual lakefronts with the south end of town touching the north shore of Skaha Lake, and the north end of town lying along the southern tip of 70-mile-long Lake Okanagan. The weather was beautiful.

The Okanagan Valley, stretching from Osoyoos at the United States border north to Vernon, is almost dry enough to be called a desert in some areas with tumbleweed blowing in the breeze. There is great variety in its climate and landscape. The valley is laden with orchards, making it especially appealing in spring when the fruit trees are in full bloom. Cherries, peaches, pears, apricots, plums, apples, and grapes are grown in the orchards and vineyards and some of the best fruit- and vegetable-growing land in the world is found here. There are breathtaking landscapes with mountains, valleys and lakes. When driving in the Knox Mountain Nature Park in Kelowna, you can see, at a depth of 25 feet a replica of Ogopogo, a mythological creature reputed to inhabit the waters of nearby Okanagan Lake.

S. S. Sicamous, a sternwheeler steamboat previously used for shipping fruits and vegetables, is now preserved as a restaurant on the beach at Penticton. We visited the Okanagan Game Farm with lions, zebra, camels, tigers, mountain goats, and many other animals.

After enjoying a wonderful Feast, Don came to our motel to take us back with him to Calgary, Alberta. It was a scary drive through the Rocky Mountains because it rained most of the way and was also foggy. You could hardly see where you were driving, let alone see other cars. Visibility was about zero! However, we arrived safely and spent a few days holidaying in Calgary, before returning home.

In June 1987, Willie came on another visit from England. He stayed about a week here in St. Catharines before going to other areas of Canada, including New Liskeard, Ontario and Vancouver, British Columbia. He visited with Shirley and Barbara in Hamilton, cousin Bob Todd in Rockwood, and with the McKay family in British Columbia. Willie and I had much more time to reminisce this time. We looked at photographs I had and the memories flowed. It was a real bonding time for us to help make up for the many years we had been apart.

Jane's family in the United States were having a reunion in Wisconsin Dells at the Feast in 1988, and asked us to join them. This was a time I will never forget. We travelled from Canboro to Buffalo to stay two days with Jane's sister. Then we all flew together from there. It was necessary for me to pack three different bags of clothes, one for Buffalo (to be left there until our return), one to carry on the plane, in case our luggage went astray, and one for the Feast. Our first destination, the huge O'Hara Airport in Chicago, was so congested they delayed our Buffalo plane from leaving for half an hour or more. When we arrived late at O'Hara, our next plane was almost ready to leave. The airlines give wings to small children. Jane had forgotten to ask the stewardess for Tania's wings so she went back on the plane to get them. We waited, and finally Bill went to look for Jane. We waited some more until Dennis said, "We'll miss our plane, because we have to walk half way across the airport." So he went in search of Bill and Jane to hurry them up. Debbie, carrying her boy, Garrat, and myself, carrying Tania became anxious so we set off on our own to get the next plane. The others didn't know where we had gone, talk about confusing! Anyway they followed and caught up to us at the door of the plane, where a man was trying to rush us aboard. Boy, were we ever exhausted! We just flopped into our seats and the plane took off. The weather became stormy and the flight was a bit bumpy but we arrived safely. We had a wonderful feast, a great reunion with Jane's family and enjoyed the attractions in Wisconsin and other areas.

At Lost Canyon we enjoyed the tour riding through a magnificent mile of cliff-walled gorges in a comfortable and quaint horse-drawn carriage. Lost Canyon is a natural wonder. There is a tree shaped like a wishbone—of course, it has been named The Wishbone Tree.

We had a ride on a steam train at North Freedom. The depot was constructed in 1894 by the Chicago and North Western Railway at Rock Springs, Wisconsin. The building was donated in 1963 and moved to the Museum and restored. The depot has two waiting rooms separated by the ticket office and a freight room on the end now occupied by the Museum gift shop.

The House on the Rock is an architectural marvel designed and built by Alex Jordan. There is a huge carousel, the largest in the world, with 269 carousel figures and over 18,000 lights. There are magnificent music machines and electronic symphonies that fill entire rooms; a gas lit "Main" street recreating the 1880's; two revolving doll carousels. In the Circus Building there is a collection of miniature circuses with delicately hand-crafted circus costumes, an animated circus band and symphony, as well as a life-size pyramid of fiberglass elephants. In the Oriental Room there are beautifully carved elephant tusks, hand-carved cork exhibits, detailed replicas of the crown Jewels, armour made especially for The House On The Rock and beautifully cased guns. There are collections of stained glass, bronze statuary, music machines, antique guns, mechanical banks, dolls and doll houses, ivory and cork carvings, oriental art, porcelain and ceramics and unique gardens.

We had a ride on a Wisconsin Duck Amphibious "boat" that goes on land and on the water of Lake Delton.

Stand Rock is a unique table of rock that is almost 20 feet in diameter across the top, stands 40 feet high, and has a gap of about six feet from the cliff.

In 1990 we went to the Feast of Tabernacles in Big Sandy, Texas, where Jane's sister Betty lived. We took the Delta flight from Buffalo, New York, to Atlanta, Georgia, then transferred to another plane for Dallas. Upon arriving there we rented a car and drove to Big Sandy. The Bowers camped out in the Piney Woods and we stayed in their home. The weather was hot and some days humid, but I enjoyed it just the same.

Many buildings on the campus were in various stages of being built in preparation for the combining of the Pasadena and Big Sandy Ambassador Colleges. The Big Sandy campus opened in 1964 with 150 students was on 1,600 acres in east Texas. The large Field House and the Redwood Building, now the library, stood as permanent structures. Meals and meetings were held in the Redwood Building. Classes met in buildings intended for short-term use, until permanent classrooms could be constructed. Until dormitories could be built, students slept in temporary metal booths. The original campus grounds were donated by Buck Hammer in 1952. That original acreage now comprised the college entrance, the college library and the lower valley area. The area was a combination of pine forest and underbrush, liberally infested with snakes and insects, and practically impassable. With vision and hard work, workers carved out a college campus amongst rolling hills, flowing streams and tall pine trees. The campus expanded to 2,200 acres to meet the growing needs of the college. The Field House was renovated to accommodate an increased student body. New classrooms were added and the student dining hall was expanded.

On December 14, 1989, Chancellor Joseph W. Tkach announced that the College's board of regents had reached a decision to consolidate the California and Texas four-year liberal arts programs of Ambassador College at the Big Sandy, Texas, campus. The move was fully implemented in August, 1990. A new lecture hall, hall of administration and new student residence halls were built to aid the expansion of the College.

Annie's Tea room was a lovely place for a delicious breakfast. Over 500 animals are on display year round at the Caldwell Zoo in Tyler, Texas. Giraffes graze on the pasture lands of the African veldt with elephants nearby.

After the Feast we were able to visit Jefferson, Texas. There was much to see and do there, wish we had more time. Perhaps one day we can make another trip to this beautiful state. We took a tour of historical Jefferson in a horse drawn wagon and took a one-hour trip on the bayou, down the steamboat passage that once connected Jefferson with Shreveport and New Orleans, Louisiana.

I travelled with Bill, Jane and family to Lexington, Kentucky, to keep the Feast of Tabernacles in 1992. On October 8, we left St. Catharines at four o'clock in the morning, stopping at eight for breakfast at the Diamond Restaurant in Richmond Heights, Ohio. Leaving at 10 a.m. we reached the Holiday Inn, Columbus, Ohio by 12:30 p.m. This was to be our stop over for the night; we had supper at the Atrium Restaurant. By 7:30 the next morning, we were on our way again, arriving in Crescent Springs just beyond Cincinnati by 10:30 where we enjoyed a lovely breakfast at Bob Evans Restaurant. Continuing the journey we reached our destination, French Quarter Suites Hotel, Lexington, Kentucky by 2:15 p.m., where we met the Knaaks, and Hussaks, and later the Bowers and Jack and Virginia Greathouse because this was a reunion for Jane's family.

We visited Fort Boonesborough State Park in Richmond, Kentucky. There is a monument dedicated to the memory of the brave pioneers who entered the wilderness of what later became Kentucky and formed the settlement of Boonesborough, the first fortified settlement in Kentucky. The Transylvania Company organized by Richard Henderson in North Carolina purchased the land south of the Kentucky River from the Cherokee Indians for resale to settlers. Daniel Boone was hired to lead the Transylvania Company expedition into Kentucky, claim it and build a fort. The fort was built under his direction according to Henderson's plan during the spring and summer of 1775. The fort withstood assaults by formidable bodies of Indians on April 16 and July 6, 1777 and August 8, 1778. The fort was reconstructed on this site which overlooks the original site on the Kentucky River to commemorate the courage of Daniel Boone, the pioneers he led, the Indians they fought and the contribution the fort made to the settling of this country. There were antiques and pioneer crafts on display—weaving and spinning, homemade soap, hand-dipped candles, baskets, brooms, toys, pottery.

The Mary Todd Lincoln house is located in Lexington Kentucky. Mary Todd Lincoln was a member of a prominent Kentucky family and wife of Abraham Lincoln, 16th President of the United States. Her girlhood home provides a glimpse of her early years and of the lifestyle of the Todd family. Mary Todd's father, Robert Todd, while trained as a lawyer, was primarily a businessman. A contemporary of John Wesley Hunt and Henry Clay, Todd served as president of the Lexington branch Bank of Kentucky and was a member of the Kentucky General Assembly for 24 years. In the early 1830s, Robert Todd renovated a brick tavern that had been constructed in 1803, on West Main Street, into an elegant single-family residence. The two-story, brick, late-Georgian house, was a suitable residence for the

Todd family, which eventually included 16 children. In 1832, Robert Todd moved his family, including his daughter Mary. Mary was born in 1818, was well-educated, attended private schools in Lexington where she learned to speak fluent French, acquired the necessary social graces and heard the political issues of the day. In 1839, Mary Todd moved to Springfield, Illinois, to live with her sister, Elizabeth Todd Edwards. There she met, and in 1842 married attorney and political figure Abraham Lincoln. Later, the Lincolns would visit Mary's girlhood house, where Lincoln spent hours enjoying the many books in Robert Todd's library. At the death of Robert Todd in 1849, an inventory of the contents of his home was made. Today, this inventory has proven invaluable in the refurnishing of the house after its restoration in 1977.

Lexington is the horse capital of the world with thoroughbred racing in April and October. The Circus Flora was enjoyed with music, clowns, juggling, pirates, high wire acts, and more. Tania and Wende had pony rides; there are beautiful sculptures of horses at Thoroughbred Park; and there was fun for the children, both small and big at Lexington Children's Museum.

For the return journey on October 20, we left Lexington, Kentucky at 10 a.m., reached Mansfield, Ohio at 2 p.m. where we toured the town for half an hour before our lunch at Bob Evans Restaurant. We resumed our journey, stopping near Medina to do some shopping, then travelled onward. Along the way light snow was visible here and there in the fields. The weather was not good, it was raining and turning nasty. We stopped at 7:30 p.m. at Travelodge in Beachwood, Ohio for the night. We left at 9:30 in the morning and arrived at Nanny and Jack's home (Jane's parents) in Allegany, New York at quarter to one. We stayed with them for two nights, doing some shopping during the day in Olean, a short distance away. On October 23rd we left Allegany, stopped at the Arcade, ate at Pizza Hut in Hamburg, and arrived in St. Catharines at 4 p.m.

I attended the Feast of Tabernacles in 1993 in Saratoga Springs, New York. I visited the Lake George Zoological Park, Catskill, New York with Bill, Jane and the granddaughters. I visited Quad/Graphics in Saratoga Springs where several international editions of The Plain Truth magazine is printed, including the Canadian English language edition. The Martins were also at Saratoga Springs.

We visited Fort William Henry Museum and restoration—the French & Indian War 1755-1757—site of James Fenimore Cooper's classic "The Last of the Mohicans". Fort William Henry was constructed at the southern end of Lake George in 1755 by Major-General William Johnson and a group of Colonial volunteers. The British military strategists designed the fort to be a key installation in the northern defense of the colony of New York. It was to serve as a launching point for future military operations against the threatening French empire to the north. The fort guarded the portage between waters on Lake George and the Hudson River to prevent any large scale French invasion. This portage was a vital link in the water route from Montreal to New York City. Formed by the St. Lawrence and Richelieu Rivers, Lake Champlain, Lake George, and the Hudson River, this historic "Warpath of the Nations" provided an avenue over which the French and British armies and their Indian allies moved in their military operations for the conquest of North America.

The Fort was constructed during the armed prelude to the final colonial conflict between France and England in the New World. It served His Britanic Majesty in the French and Indian War which marked the culmination of a century of struggle for the control of the North American Continent that saw the English emerge supreme.

When Johnson arrived in the area during the month of September, he found an armed force ready to maintain the French title by open conflict. The opposing armies vied for control of the land in an engagement known as the Battle of Lake George. The fighting took place in an area east of the fort at the present site of Lake George State Park. The British under Johnson and their Mohawk allies under Chief "King" Hendrick, narrowly gained a victory over the French under Barton de Dieskau.

Following the battle, Johnson assigned his Chief engineer, Captain William Eyre, the task of designing a formal fort. The survivors of the battle exchanged their muskets for hammers and saws and began construction of the log fortress. Through the efforts of the volunteer soldiers from this and the surrounding colonies, the fort began to take life. Johnson christened Fort William Henry in honour of two royal grandsons of King George II.

Because of Fort William Henry, the residents of the entire colony slept more peacefully knowing that there was protection against Indian raiding parties. The true hour of destiny for the fort came in 1757. During that turbulent year, the fort twice repulsed the French military machine. The first attack was launched against it in the winter of that year by a French force of 1,500 regulars and their Huron allies, led by Sieur de Riguad de Vaudreuil. For protection from the extreme cold, the French troops built camp fires which revealed their position to the British pickets and prevented the French from staging a surprise attack on the garrison at Fort William Henry. When the opposing army reached the fort, it was met by a withering fire from the British troops and finally driven off after they had nearly succeeded in firing the fort by igniting nearby buildings. A heavy snowfall the very night of the attempted burning helped to quench the flames and prevent the fort's complete destruction. Vaudreuil was forced to withdraw his troops and retire through deep snow drifts back to Fort Carillon at Ticonderoga.

In August of 1757, the most brilliant French General of the Colonial period, the Marquis de Montcalm, sailed up Lake George with a force of 8,000 crack French regulars, a large party of Indian allies, and Canadian volunteers. Montcalm deployed his troops and artillery train of thirty-two pieces. Once their cannons were in siege position, the French expected the fort to surrender rather than engage such an impressive army in battle. When an easy capitulation was not forthcoming, Montcalm initiated a brutal assault with great vigor and much skill. The defending garrison, under the command of Lieutenant-Colonel George Munro, consisted of 2,200 men. In addition, there were numerous women and children from neighbouring settlements who sought refuge within the safety of the fort's walls. After a siege of six days, Colonel Munro realized that the structure of the fort was near collapse and he surrendered.

We kept the Feast of Tabernacles in London, Ontario at the London Convention Centre from September 27 to October 5, 1996. We went to the Western Imax Theatre to see "The Secret of Life on Earth" on October 2. The film is shown on a giant screen five storeys high. We soared over majestic mountain ranges and vast rain forest canopies, peered through the underbrush at the inner workings of the deadly Venus Flytrap, showing the interdependence between plants, animals and other forms of life. The film conveys the simple truth: plants give us life . . . and they help us keep it. "The Dream is Alive" on October 3 was film footage shot by 14 NASA astronauts on three separate space shuttle missions showing the splendour of earth from 250 miles up

London Regional Children'sMuseum was visited where the children could "dig for dinosaurs, journey to the stars, and crawl through caves". At the London Museum of Archaeology, thousands of years of history of occupation of Southwestern Ontario is presented, including Lawson Prehistoric Indian village. We went inside the old London Court House and Gaol in the Middlesex County Building. First Hussars Museum is located in the Middlesex County Building and it was interesting to see memoirs of the First Hussars Regiment.

Chapter 20

Coins of Gold Flying From the Pouch

Many lines of prose,
I can often compose,
When trying to doze!
This verse is one of those!

Don't ask how or why
The words come floating by,
As in bed I lie
Trying sleep not to deny!

These thoughts of mine
Often come in line!
And if they seem fine,
To them, my name I'll sign!

Both of my sisters,
Have very fine misters!
And from much hard work
Have gotten many blisters!

> Better looking by far,
> Than brothers you are!
> You must have been born
> Under a very lucky star!
>
> Barbara Jean and Shirley May,
> I love you much today
> And will think of you often
> When I'm gone away!
>
> Now this silly little ditty
> May not seem very witty!
> But it's over now,
> Ain't that a pity!
>
> James Cromwell
> April 9, 2007

The time passed so quickly and before we knew it, our family had grown and were about to start leaving us. On July 22, 1972 Rodney Stewart married Jenny Mans with the service in a church in Dunnville and the reception at the Mans' home. Rodney and Jenny took up residence in Dunnville.

Barbara followed the next month when she married Harry Raué on August 13, 1972, in West Flamborough. The town hall was the location for the ceremony performed by George Menassas. Pictures were taken at Webster's Falls and the reception was held at the town hall with about 80 guests. Barbara had previously gone to work in Hamilton and was living there with a church family, Klaus and Judy Brandt. Harry and Barbara honeymooned in western Canada. They lived in Hamilton.

On February 4, 1974 Zane Andrew Raué was born. He was my first grandchild and I spent the first week helping to look after him.

Jennifer Lorraine Lynn Stewart was born May 9, 1974.

Don and Bill did some work for Mr. Russ McQuillen and then went to work for Wayne Minor at the Canborough Feed Mill. Cleason was working there, so they rented a house next door to the mill and lived together. Don had a hankering to go to western Canada and when Jim was out of work in 1974, they headed for the West. They saw beaver and grizzly bears among other animals at the Assiniboine Zoo in Winnipeg (September 14), buffalo at Lake Rudy, Manitoba (September 15), visited Calgary's Dinosaur Park (September 20), Sunwapta Falls and River in Jasper Park (September 24). They saw the Three Sisters located on the edge of Canmore Town site, an unusual group of peaks in the Rocky Mountains aptly named. Guarding the entrance to Banff National Park, these mountains have often been used as a landmark of the area. Banff, with Mt. Rundle in the background, is considered one of Canada's most scenic views and can be seen from the Banff cable car lift on Mt. Norquay which has an elevation of 6900 feet. Lake Louise is one and a half miles long and three quarters of a mile wide, is 273 feet deep and the temperature of the water is a mere 20 degrees above freezing even in the warmest weather. Located in a bowl-shaped valley, Lake Louise is one of the most beautiful, awe inspiring sights in the Canadian Rockies, with Victoria Glacier at one end. Moraine Lake lies in the valley of the Ten Peaks and is one of the beautiful gems of the Rocky Mountains. The lake was formed by landslides of rock from near the Tower of Babel. The Tower of Babel is a quartzite outlier of Mount Babel, and is adjacent to the rockslide (originally thought to be a moraine) that terminates Moraine Lake in the Valley of the Ten Peaks. It is one of the earliest rock climbing venues in the Lake Louise area, but has now largely fallen out of fashion in favour of the crags at the "back end" of Lake Louise. Don and Jim were in Vancouver on the Capilano suspension bridge on September 27, 1974.

Jim worked as a trainer on the Calgary and Edmonton tracks, until he got a job with Mid-West Drilling.

In the meantime Shirley went to Hamilton to work for the Taxation Office and she also lived with the Brandts. On June 29, 1975 Shirley married Edward Martin at Ohsweken and took up residence in Hamilton. After Dad had escorted Shirley up the aisle, he had an angina attack, and I had to leave the wedding and go to Hagersville hospital with him. He was put in intensive care. It was very hard for Orlin to see all the children go, all the golden coins leaving the pouch.

Michael Duane was born March 19, 1977 to Harry and Barbara, their second son. On February 24, 1978, Kevin Rodney was born, now one girl and one boy for Rodney and Jenny. Ed and Shirley had a boy, Brandon *Lance*, born July 20, 1979. Randy Nolan Martin was born on March 14, 1982, making two boys for Ed and Shirley.

It was lonely with Orlin gone and all the children living away from me, but there was always work to be done. I planted a garden each year and spent many hours every week cutting the great expanse of lawn that we had. There was a purpose for me staying there. Cleason began courting a girl from the United States. In order for them to get to know each other better she came up and stayed at my place. On September 30, 1984 Cleason married Joan Bernice Dzubella in an outdoor ceremony in North Evans, New York, U.S.A. They went to live in Canborough, Ontario. Don came home for the wedding.

Bill began courting an American girl and my home was again used for the same purpose as before. Bill married Nora *Jane* Bragg on September 1, 1985 in Hamburg, New York.

I moved to my apartment at 64 Windward Street in St. Catharines, Ontario on October 10, 1985. It is a nice building in the north part of the city. From my window and balcony on the fourth floor, I could see the ships passing through the Welland Ship Canal. I am close to Lock 2.

Though not brought up in the country, through living in the Dunnville area so long I had grown to love it. Now I missed not being able to walk out into the fields. I spent quite a bit of my summers visiting Shirley in Oakville, Barbara in Hamilton, and especially Bill and Jane in Canborough. I like to be with my grandchildren as much as possible while they are very young, coins of gold in my pouch.

Annette Michelle Margreta Raué was born to Harry and Barbara on September 30, 1983, making three in their family. While spending time with Barbara and the new baby, I helped choose her name.

During my 1987 holiday at Shirley's, we made a sentimental journey to Guelph, visiting the area of our former home, the O.R. where the kids used to swim, and Riverside Park where we had a picnic lunch. Shirley also saw two schools she had attended.

Tania Leila Cromwell was born to Bill and Jane on April 30, 1988. She was my first grandchild with red hair, a beautiful baby. You can be sure I stayed a while at their home. I decided at this time to buy a camera so that I could get a lot of pictures of my grandchildren.

In the spring of 1992, I received some wonderful news. James, my oldest son, phoned to say he was getting married to Mary Ann Henschel in August. Immediately, upon informing the family, Bill, Shirley and I decided to attend the wedding. On August 1st Shirley, Bill and I travelled to Pearson International Airport where we boarded an Air Canada flight to Winnipeg, Manitoba. Upon arriving, I looked for someone wearing a western hat but neither Don nor James was wearing one. It was a happy meeting for us because I had not seen James since Bill was married in 1985. Don took us to Mary Ann's house, where we were staying.

We talked long into the night. Next morning, after breakfast and snapping pictures, Don took us to see some sights in Winnipeg. Don took us along Main Street where I had lived in 1949. I tried to pick out the house, which was next to a store, and saw one that might have been it, but I'm not sure because I had forgotten the number. We passed by the entrance to Kildonan Park, which I noticed is different now from the picture I took of it in 1949. Some things change over the years and others do not.

The wedding was at 6 p.m. I was told that the bride would be wearing leopard skin. Imagine the thoughts that were going through my mind at this moment!! What kind of wedding would this be? Well, my fears were put to rest when the bride and groom greeted and welcomed us into the hall. She wasn't wearing a leopard skin, per se, but had a leopard skin motif on the top she wore over her dress. One of her friends had it on her blouse while the other one wore a leopard skin skirt. It certainly was different, but they looked very nice. After the delicious meal, people came forward to explain various articles on a memorabilia table. Dancing followed and wedding cake and other desserts were served later. On August 8th, the family gathered at Ed and Shirley's in Oakville. The newlyweds, with Don and Marlene, were to meet us there for a family reunion. The last time we were all together was in 1973, a period of nineteen years.

When a delicious supper was ended and more pictures were taken, Don and Marlene, James and Mary Ann and I travelled to Hamilton to stay the night at the Raués. The next morning we went to Niagara-on-the-Lake for lunch and shopping in the stores, then on to Niagara Falls for the rest of the day. In the evening we ate supper at the Turf and Surf, one of our favourite eating places. Upon returning to their Motel, we said our good-byes to the boys and their wives, who would stay overnight in Niagara Falls, then head back to Winnipeg by way of the United States the next day.

On Wednesday, August 19, 1992, Barbara and I went on a trip. The first stop was Moffat, where we lived when her father died in 1955. Findlay's garage on the corner of Regional Road 15 is now an outlet for selling jams and preserves. Tom Moffat occupies the house we lived in which was next door, on the sideroad. He is the son of Del and Doris Moffat who owned the store. Doris' mother was Mrs. Ellsley. Another Ellsley's had a large store in Campbellville. A widow, Mrs. Donevan, lived next to us. When our pump was broken she let me get water from her well. Then next was Charlie Robert's house which is now an antique store. He once did some carpentry work for me. The Dobbs' farm is still there but the front part of the land where the entrance was now contains houses. We found the new entrance on the main road where we had first come into Moffat. Violet Dobbs or her daughter Jean babysat for me whenever I went into town to shop and especially after my husband died and I was looking to buy a home in Guelph. When we moved, Jean came with us to help me unpack and get settled into our new home on Old York Road.

Frank and Aggie Hathaway's house opposite the garage is gone. He worked on the railroad and always kept his clocks on railroad time. Daylight Saving Time did not exist for him. I saw what was once the Allens' summer house. I used their well sometimes to get water. At the Post Office, formerly Del Moffatt's store, we met John Moore who lives two doors away. He has been in Moffatt since 1947 and invited us in for a cup of coffee. The old Post Office that I knew was on one side of the railway tracks and the train station was on the other side; both of these buildings were torn down. Josh Allison was the postmaster then. People on the main road had to pick up their mail but those of us on the side roads had mail box delivery. The railway tracks remain and the caution signals were flashing while a few cars were being shunted back and forth as I watched from the Dents home. The Dents moved to Moffatt shortly after we left in the spring of 1956. They gave us much information about various people in the area and showed us a book on Nassagaweya township. About four trains a day would stop at the station to take people in and out of Guelph, which was quite handy for me. But there was talk at that time about cutting the train service altogether. We moved before that happened.

We found the school that Jim attended in Grade 1, S.S. No. 3 Nassagaweya Township. It is now a house but still has the name in the stonework on the front, with the year the school was built, 1870.

Barbara and I had a picnic lunch alongside the country road outside Moffatt. Then we headed for Ospringe. My cousin Rosa's husband, Carl Saillian, had a farm near there, to which I came when I returned from England in 1948. We went to see the old farm home and to take some pictures. A girl there informed us that the house was about 150 years old and the barn 100 years old. The original barn had burned down. Barbara also took a picture of me standing on the same bridge where I had my picture taken in the spring of 1948.

We had supper in Guelph and a walking tour down Wyndham Street before returning to Hamilton.

On October 18, 1994, Aimee Elizabeth May Cromwell was born to Bill and Jane, making three daughters in their family.

Chapter 21

Celebrations

In May 1991, I began writing the "Memories of My Life", although I didn't then have that title in mind. This story was prompted by my daughter Barbara, who had given me, The Story of My Life, from things I had said over the years and from her viewpoint. I thought it would be better if I wrote it myself and besides I had a lot more to tell than she knew about. I began by jotting down some things of yester-year that came to my mind and so the story grew from there. On May 27, I went to Barbara's home in Hamilton and she began putting what I had written into the computer.

On June 17, Joan and I arose early in the morning and started on our journey to my old hometown of Belleville. My last time there was in 1932 when we moved to Malverne and then left for England. The city has grown in all those years but the house I lived in is still there, although somewhat altered.

We visited the school I attended until 1932 and it is much the same as it was then. Only two of the older schools are still in use, Queen Victoria Public, mine, and Belleville Collegiate Institute. The Principal of Q.V.P., from his office, saw us taking a picture of the school and came out to talk to us. He invited us into the school where he gave me a sketch and a crest, marking the seventy-fifth anniversary of the school in 1987. He told me that my records and marks are there somewhere in the basement of the school. He also took us into the auditorium, which is kept locked up. It is just as it was years ago.

Joan and I walked on the sand dune at Sandbanks Provincial Park. Joan and I were having such a wonderful time that we stayed four days.

In August, Barbara, Annette and I took a trip to Guelph. We visited Riverside Park with the floral clock and swinging bridge, the John McCrae Memorial, the Ontario Reformatory Grounds. We visited Donna Cromwell's sister Jean and Carl and Rosa Saillian.

We visited S.S. No. 1 Guelph Township School where all five children went up to Grade 6. James attended MacDonald Consolidated for Grades 7 and 8; Barbara went there for Grade 7; Donald went there for Grade 6. Barbara was at College Avenue Public School for Grade 8, Don was there for Grade 7, Shirley was there for Grades 5 and 6, Bill was there for Grade 5. James attended four years at John F. Ross Collegiate Vocational Institute, as did Barbara (except for the last month and a half at Dunnville District Secondary School).

On Sunday, December 22, 1991 the family gathered together at Bill and Jane's home in Canboro for a delicious turkey dinner. After the meal, I made an important announcement to the family gathered in the living room. Here it is: "Family members, this is the moment you have been waiting for. I hope you will not be disappointed. I now present to you my book, "Memories of My Life"." I call, "Bill" and hand the first volume to him. Bill says, "Is this all there is?" Then opening the curtain between the dining room and kitchen I say, "And here is the rest of my book!" The six grandchildren enter, one at a time, carrying the remaining ten volumes. Champagne is opened and the adults have a toast. Barbara and I signed the first book. Then the grandchildren distributed the books to the family members and others present. The family spent a lot of time looking at and reading portions of the many volumes of my book. It made me feel very happy to have accomplished this tremendous job of writing my life history.

75th

Shirley phoned to ask if I would like to come over on February 19, 1995. I had an inkling, in the back of my mind, that something was going on, because this was the week of my 75th birthday. But everyone acted so naturally that I just put the thoughts aside. Even my little granddaughters, Tania and Wende, kept the secret perfectly.

We had lunch and were sitting in the living room talking, when one of Ed's brothers, with his wife and family, a nephew and Ed's mother, paid an unexpected visit. After serving coffee and tea, Shirley asked if I had been in the basement to see the changes that were made. Bill led me and a few of the guests downstairs to take a look. I noticed the wallboard that partitioned off the laundry room. Then I opened the door into the recreation room, before remembering that a boarder now lived there. Well, she was away for the weekend so we went in and inspected the new paneling on one wall which had not been done when I was last there. Having been told we couldn't come up yet, Bill and I sat on the couch and Bill started quoting scripture to me. Ha! Ha! All this time, it was really only about five or ten minutes, I can imagine people were working frantically upstairs to get everything in place.

Upon reaching the top of the stairs and coming through the door, I was surprised to see my other daughter Barbara and Jane holding cameras high in the air, ready to snap my startled look! Wow! What a surprise!

There was a huge Happy Birthday sign over top of the glass door, balloons floating over a table with another sign "75", and presents and cards galore. I had figured they were putting on a nice supper for me but I never dreamed of anything like this! And best of all, my whole family (those who live in Ontario) were all there.

It was time to open the presents and cards. I invited Tania and Wende to help and Annette kept track of "who gave me what." I think they were very excited too! The family seemed to know everything I needed or wanted because that's what I received (maybe they read my little notes that I leave on the counter).

We sat down to a delicious supper of some of my favourite foods. Mmm mmm, was it ever good and all prepared by my loving daughters and daughters-in-law. The 75th Birthday Party was to give thanks and to honour Mom/Grandma for reaching her 75th birthday—Sunday, February 19, 1995—at Ed and Shirley Martin's home. Menu: broccoli soup, cabbage rolls, lasagna, mashed potatoes, broccoli with cheese sauce, cauliflower with cheese sauce, corn, tossed salad, cabbage salad, whole wheat buns, wine, punch, tea, pop; dessert: butter tarts, lemon pie, key lime pie, nanaimo bars and birthday cake. What a lovely day it was and what a wonderful family God has given to me. I am truly blessed.

On the morning of my actual birthday, February 23rd, a lovely bouquet of flowers arrived from James and Mary Ann. Upon returning from school, Joan drove me to the Pen Centre to pick up my Sears order, then we headed for Niagara Falls. After viewing the Falls in all its icy splendour, Joan took me to the Falls Manor Family Restaurant, where we enjoyed a delicious fish and chip dinner.

The 19th and 23rd of February, 1995 are two days that I will remember for a long time. Some days later, Don phoned from Calgary to ask me how I felt, at age 75, and to wish me a happy birthday. That made my joy complete because now, all of my family had remembered.

Mom's 80th

Born but once to this life,
Anniversaries of that occasion,
Give one reason to ponder and remember,
Years of good times with great elation.

Surrounded by family and friends
All wishing you the very best;
They've come from all around,
Even sons from the far west!

With sons and daughters, in-laws too;
Many grandchildren, big and small,
Each bringing to your thoughts
Different memories of them all.

More distant in miles than some,
Tho' not as far as Don and Marlene,
James and Mary Ann (and Johnny, too);
Loving thoughts keep us closer than is seen.

First, with time together sadly shortened,
There were five with Oliver,
Then, with Orlin and S.C. #9,
You added Cleason and Rodney together.

Now Barbara and Harry married,
And then there were grandchildren three:
Zane and Michael and Annette:
Also, with two, were Rodney and Jenny.

Shirley and Ed, with Lance and Randy,
Soon gave you two grandsons.
And along the way,
The marriage of Joan and Cleason's.

Close to home, Bill and Jane,
And three granddaughters fine:
Tania, Wende and Aimee also;
Your life is now very divine.

All this extended family,
With love and devotion:
Who've provided memories numerous,
Fill this day with emotion.

       James Cromwell

    * * *

On Saturday, February 19, 2000, family and friends gathered together at Bill and Jane Cromwell's, 46 Lyons Avenue East, Welland, Ontario for my 80th birthday. Hors d'oeuvres and beverages were available. I was quite surprised when I walked in and saw my sons James and Don sitting on the couch—that had been kept secret. I received birthday congratulations from Jean Chretien, Prime Minister of Canada, Tim Hudak, MPP Erie-Lincoln, Michael D. Harris, Premier of Ontario, and Peter Kormos, MPP Niagara Centre. Many nice gifts were given to me along with a lot of love from those who came; a very rewarding day!

Mom's Birthday Bash

It was a great surprise,
You could see it in her eyes
When Mom came through the door
To see friends and family galore!

They came from far and near;
To help our Mother so dear,
Celebrate this occasion fine,
With fellowship, food and wine.

Five sons and daughters on hand;
Of your life's time, a big demand.
Not to mention would never do:
Four in-laws there, too!

All your grandsons there to see,
Zane and Michael, Lance and Randy.
And granddaughters all so lovely!
Annette and Tania, Wende and Aimee!

Many other friends there were;
'Tho mostly to me a blur:
To your memory they bring,
Thoughts to make your heart sing.

Thanks to all who participated
And made Mom so elated!
Also to those not able to share:
'Cause we know how much you care.

Mom, we do love you dearly,
'Tho not always seen yearly!
Happy to have been with you,
For this 80th birthday do!

By James Cromwell

I enjoyed the visit of James and Don from the west for a few more days until they had to return home.

Chapter 22

Goodbye, Mom

Mom, a small word but she meant a lot to us.

In the early 1990's, I worked with Mom to help her write a story of her life which she called her memories. She bound the work in photo albums and presented them to the family in December 1995.

Over the past two years we talked to Mom about completing the story of the next twelve years of her life to add to the photos she kept organized in the albums—always right up-to-date! Last summer Mom and I began that process when she came over to Dundas for a week's holiday. After her return home, she carried on and wrote more. I received the latest update in December 2006.

Mom's children and grandchildren now have that visual memory of Mom and the times in which she lived.

Mom loved to do scrapbooks: the Dionne Quintuplets and Movie Stars were her very early ones before her trip to England where she lived during World War II. She has been working on scrapbooks this past winter on Tiger Woods, Movie Stars, wild animals and scenery. We found out only a few years ago that Mom loved pictures of wild animals, and especially liked elephants—she received quite a collection of elephants in different sizes and poses from that point onward.

When Mom came to our place for a visit, the first place she would head to was the garden to see what flowers were blooming. Raspberries, strawberries and currants were searched for on the bushes for a mixed fresh fruit bowl most days of her visits.

Mom spent hours working on jigsaw puzzles. Her favourite ones were glued on boards and displayed around the walls of her apartment, with wild animals, flowers and scenery being her favourite ones.

Mom loved old movies and had a collection of hundreds of them. Biographies of movie stars was another interest of hers. She loved to sing and had favourite singers from the past. She enjoyed Glenn Miller band music, among others.

Mom raised five children on her own—the youngest, William, was born 1½ months after Dad was killed in a work accident. As a widow, Mom bought a house, financed it and paid for it in twelve years.

She was the only mother in the neighbourhood who took time to play with the children—baseball, tin can cricket, watched us swim at the lake on the Ontario Reformatory grounds and at Riverside Park. We played indoor games as a family as well: crokinole, canasta and other card games, hockey, ping pong using the kitchen and dining room tables pushed together with the net strung across the middle between the doorways. Cribbage is a game she enjoyed right up to 2007.

Many of Mom's interests have been passed on to her children and grandchildren. Several enjoy working on jigsaw puzzles, some enjoy the glued puzzles, some enjoy scrapbooking in our own unique ways. Board and card games are enjoyed by many. Collections of all kinds are kept.

. . . all part of Mom's legacy to us . . .

Barbara (Cromwell) Raué

MOM

Mom raised five kids with no complaint
She really was a blessed saint

She was the best we could ask for
Taught, loved us, couldn't ask for more

She taught us manners, respect and morals too
She instilled them in us through and through

On her face was always a smile
She always went that extra mile

Our special times included puzzle making
Sometimes it was quite the undertaking

She loved to bake the boys a pie
It was so nice to hear them sigh

Stop everything it's time for tea
It's something that simply had to be

Many memories will be held so dear
Close to my heart, oh so near

She amazed me right up to the end
There's nothing more that can be penned

Mom has a special place in my heart
From there I know she'll never depart

Shirley Martin (April 9, 2007)

The last, most difficult thing for us is to look into our mother's empty apartment, the furniture all taken away, the walls and floors bare. It makes her death final, a period placed at the end of a sentence, a door shutting, a light going out. Everything that had been her, that had kept her memory vivid in our minds and in our senses, is gone from these rooms, the rooms where she did her thinking, her dreaming, her scrapbooks, where she watched her movies and television shows, where she worked on her puzzles, where she sat back and admired the colourful works of art.

Goodbye, Mom. We will continue to cherish the vivid memories we have of you and of the times spent together. We have you to share and to bring us closer together. Thank you for that.

It is only the music of the heart that brings any real comfort, and that music cannot be bought at any price. That music is the only true gift we can bestow on each other.

Barbara (April 19, 2007)

Do you remember the flannel graph stories from Chapter 1? Here is another that comes alive in brilliant colours and stirring emotions. It happened at Passover (often called Easter in our times). For the past three years, Jesus had been teaching people and healing the sick. He had many wonderful things to teach and the crowds followed him in large numbers. It was almost Passover, the time when the people remembered their ancestors being freed from slavery in Egypt and leaving on their journey to the promised land. The room has been made ready and the Passover meal has been prepared. The disciples gathered with Jesus and lounged on couches as they ate the lamb, unleavened bread and bitter herbs, talking about the long ago story that had been passed down for many generations. Do you see John and Peter, James, and Andrew? Do you see Judas? The others were all gathered around joining in the reminiscing and thinking about what might lie ahead. After the meal, they headed out to the Garden of Gethsemane, a beautiful place with flowers and trees. Can you imagine some of the colours and fragrances there might have been? There may not have been daffodils and tulips or lilies like we have in our land, but beautiful flowers just the same. It was a peaceful place to go and unwind at the end of a day. Jesus often went there with his disciples, but tonight was a different night for him. He knew tonight he would be captured and condemned to die. As a human, can you even begin to imagine what thoughts he must have had? He was in such agony that he sweat drops of blood. He prayed for strength

Coins of Gold

to make it through the coming ordeal. God gave him all the time he needed to prepare for what was to come, strengthening him. Only then did the authorities come to arrest him and take him before the Sanhedrin to be tried and condemned. He was taken to Pilate who found nothing wrong in him and wanted to release him. But the Jewish leaders wanted him dead, so Pilate gave in and ordered his crucifixion. As the pieces of the story are added to the flannel board, we can see the story unfolding. Do you see Peter standing by the fireside, denying that he knows Jesus? Do you hear the rooster crowing? Can you see the crowds lining the street as Jesus tries to carry the crossbeam for his death? He had been beaten so badly that he wasn't able to carry the wooden beam and a strong man from the crowd was pressed into service to carry it. Can you see Jesus hanging on the tree with two others hanging on crosses on either side of him? It was not an easy death to be crucified. It was horrible. There were many who taunted, many who threw stones. And then there were his followers who silently watched, unable to help, the tears running down their faces as they remembered the wonderful miracles Jesus had performed, the many stories he told to teach the people. After Jesus died, Nicodemus and Joseph of Arimathea got permission to take him off the cross and lay his body in a tomb.

Is that all there is to the story? No, there is more. Three days later, God raised Jesus from the dead! It was hard for the people to believe it. Do you remember doubting Thomas who actually had to put his fingers into the nail holes in his hands and feet before he would believe that Jesus had been raised from the dead? How skeptical would we have been? The story finishes with Jesus ascending through the clouds to join his Father in heaven. Jesus went through all of that suffering to pay the penalty for all of our sins. Now we too have the hope of eternal life.

Mom has finished her physical life on earth and awaits her future when she will be resurrected as a daughter of God. Her life on earth is over, and she leaves behind her coins of gold, spilled out of the pouch, each pursuing different paths, some coins splitting and producing more golden coins, more precious ones to one day join God's family.

155